The Perfumed Garden Of The

Shaykh Nefzawi

Sheik Nefzawi

Kessinger Publishing's Rare Reprints

Thousands of Scarce and Hard-to-Find Books
on These and other Subjects!

- Americana
- Ancient Mysteries
- Animals
- Anthropology
- Architecture
- Arts
- Astrology
- Bibliographies
- Biographies & Memoirs
- Body, Mind & Spirit
- Business & Investing
- Children & Young Adult
- Collectibles
- Comparative Religions
- Crafts & Hobbies
- Earth Sciences
- Education
- Ephemera
- Fiction
- Folklore
- Geography
- Health & Diet
- History
- Hobbies & Leisure
- Humor
- Illustrated Books
- Language & Culture
- Law
- Life Sciences

- Literature
- Medicine & Pharmacy
- Metaphysical
- Music
- Mystery & Crime
- Mythology
- Natural History
- Outdoor & Nature
- Philosophy
- Poetry
- Political Science
- Science
- Psychiatry & Psychology
- Reference
- Religion & Spiritualism
- Rhetoric
- Sacred Books
- Science Fiction
- Science & Technology
- Self-Help
- Social Sciences
- Symbolism
- Theatre & Drama
- Theology
- Travel & Explorations
- War & Military
- Women
- Yoga
- *Plus Much More!*

We kindly invite you to view our catalog list at:
http://www.kessinger.net

THE
PERFUMED
GARDEN
of the

Shaykh

Nefzawi

To the pure all things are pure.
Quoted by Sir Richard Burton in his *Arabian Nights.*

There is little of love's language that I do not know . . .
James Elroy Flecker—*Hassan.*

The best books are those which startle you by contradicting your opinions and beliefs. You learn more from your enemies than your friends.

St. John Ervine (during a broadcast talk).

CONTENTS

5

6

THE PERFUMED GARDEN

INTRODUCTION

General Remarks About Coition

Praise be given to God, who has placed man's greatest pleasure in the natural parts of woman, and has destined the natural parts of man to afford the greatest enjoyment to woman.

He has not endowed the parts of woman with any pleasurable or satisfactory feeling until the same have been penetrated by the instrument of the male; and likewise the sexual organs of man know neither rest nor quietness until they have entered those of the female.

Hence the mutual operation. There takes place between the two actors wrestlings, intertwinings, a kind of animated conflict. Owing to the contact of the lower parts of the two bellies, the enjoyment soon comes to pass. The man is at work as with a pestle, while the woman seconds him by lascivious movements; finally comes the ejaculation.

The kiss on the mouth, on the two cheeks, upon the neck, as well as the sucking up of fresh lips, are gifts of God, destined to provoke erection at the favourable moment. God also was it who has embellished the chest of the woman with breasts, has furnished her with a double chin, and has given brilliant colours to her cheeks.

He has also gifted her with eyes that inspire love, and with eye-lashes like polished blades.

He has furnished her with a rounded belly and a beautiful navel, and with a majestic crupper; and all these wonders are borne up by the thighs. It is between these latter that God has placed the arena of the combat; when the same is provided with ample flesh, it resembles the head of a lion. It is called *vulva*. Oh! how many men's deaths lie at her door? Amongst them how many heroes!

God has furnished this object with a mouth, a tongue, two lips; it is like the impression of the hoof of the gazelle in the sands of the desert.

The whole is supported by two marvellous columns, testifying to the might and the wisdom of God; they are not too long nor too short; and they are graced with knees, calves, ankles, and heels, upon which rest precious rings.

Then the Almighty has plunged woman into a sea of splendours, of voluptuousness, and of delights, and covered her with precious vestments, with brilliant girdles and provoking smiles.

So let us praise and exalt him who has created woman and her beauties, with her appetising flesh; who has given her hairs, a beautiful figure, a bosom with breasts which are swelling, and amorous ways, which awaken desires.

The Master of the Universe has bestowed upon them the empire of seduction; all men, weak or strong, are subjected to the weakness for the love of woman. Through woman we have society or dispersion, sojourn or emigration.

The state of humility in which are the hearts of those who love and are separated from the object of their love, makes their hearts burn with love's fire; they are oppressed with a feeling of servitude, contempt and misery; they suffer under the vicissitudes of their passion: and all this as a consequence of their burning desire of contact.

I, the servant of God, am thankful to him that no one can help falling in love with beautiful women, and that no one can escape the desire to possess them, neither by change, nor flight, nor separation.

I testify that there is only one God. I likewise testify as to our lord and master, Mohammed, the servant and ambassador of God, the greatest of the prophets (the benediction and pity of God be with him and with his family and disciples!). I keep prayers and benedictions for the day of retribution, that terrible moment.

The Origin of this Work

I have written this magnificent work after a small book called *The Torch of the World*, which treats of the mysteries of generation.

This latter work came to the knowledge of the Vizir of our master Abd-el-Aziz, the ruler of Tunis.

When he sent for me, and invited me pressingly to come and see him, I went forthwith, and he received me most honorably.

Three days after he came to me, and showing me my book, said, 'This is your work.' Seeing me blush, he added, 'You need not be ashamed; everything you have said in it is true; no one need be shocked at your words. Moreover, you are not the first who has treated of this matter; and I swear by God that it is necessary to know this book. It is only the shameless bore and the enemy of all science who will not read it, or make fun of it. But there are sundry things which you will have to treat about yet. I wish that you would add to the work a supplement, treating of the remedies of which you have said nothing, and adding all the facts appertaining thereto, omitting nothing.'

I replied to the Vizir: 'Oh, my master, all you have said here is not difficult to do, if it is the pleasure of God on high.'

I forthwith went to work with the composition of this book, imploring the assistance of God (may he pour his blessing on his prophet, and may happiness and pity be with him).

I have called this work *The Perfumed Garden for the Soul's Recreation* (*Er Roud el Aater p'nezaha el Khater*).

CHAPTER 1

Concerning Praiseworthy Men

Learn, O Vizir (God's blessing be upon you), that there are different sorts of men and women; that amongst these are those who are worthy of praise, and those who deserve reproach.

When a meritorious man finds himself near to women, his member grows, gets strong, vigorous and hard; he is not quick to discharge, and after the trembling caused by the emission of the sperm, he is soon stiff again.

Such a man is liked and appreciated by women; this is because the woman loves the man only for the sake of coition. His member should, therefore, be of ample dimensions and length. Such a man ought to be broad in the chest, and heavy in the crupper; he should know how to regulate his emission, and be ready as to erection; his member should reach to the end of the canal of the female, and completely fill the same in all its parts. Such an one will be well beloved by women, for, as the poet says:

I have seen women trying to find in young men
The durable qualities which grace the man of full power,
The beauty, the enjoyment, the reserve, the strength,
The full-formed member providing a lengthened coition,
A heavy crupper, a slowly coming emission,
A lightsome chest, as it were floating upon them;
The spermal ejaculation slow to arrive, so as
To furnish forth a long drawn-out enjoyment.
His member soon to be prone again for erection,
To ply the plane again and again and again on their vulvas,
Such is the man whose cult gives pleasure to women,
And who will ever stand high in their esteem.

Various Lengths of the Virile Member

The virile member, to please women, must have at most a length of the breadth of twelve fingers, or three hand-breadths, and at least six fingers, or a hand and a half breadth.

There are men with members of twelve fingers, or three hand-breadths; others of ten fingers, or two and a half hands. And others measure eight fingers, or two hands. A man whose member is of less dimensions cannot please women.

The use of Perfumes in Coition

The use of perfumes, by man as well as by woman, excites to the act of copulation. The woman, inhaling the perfumes employed by the man, becomes intoxicated; and the use of scents has often proved a strong help to man, and assisted him in getting possession of a woman.

On this subject it is told of Moçailama, the impostor, the son of Kaiss (whom God may curse!), that he pretended to have the gift of prophecy, and imitated the Prophet of God (blessings and salutations to him).

And thus acted that woman of the Beni-Temim, called *Chedjâ el Temimia,* who pretended to be a prophetess. She had heard of Moçailama, and he likewise of her.

This woman was powerful, for the Beni-Temim form a numerous tribe. She said, 'Prophecy cannot belong to two persons. Either he is a prophet, and then I and my disciples will follow his laws, or I am a prophetess, and then he and his disciples will follow my laws.'

Chedjâ then wrote to Moçailama a letter, in which she told him, 'It is not proper that two persons should at one and the same time profess prophecy. We will meet, we and our disciples, and examine each other. We shall discuss about that which has come to us from God (the Koran), and we will follow the laws of him acknowledged as the true prophet.'

She then closed her letter and gave it to a messenger, saying: 'Betake yourself, with this missive, and give it to Moçailama ben Kaiss. As for myself, I follow, with the army.'

Next day the prophetess mounted horse, with her *goum,* and followed the spoor of her envoy. When the latter arrived at Moçailama's place, he greeted him and gave him the letter.

Moçailama opened and read it, and understood its contents. He was dismayed. While he was in this perplexity, one of the superior men of his *goum* came forward and said to him: 'Oh, Moçailama, calm your soul and cool your eye. I will give you the advice of a father to his son.'

Moçailama said to him: 'Speak, and may thy words be true.'

And the other one said: 'Tomorrow morning erect outside the

12

city a tent of coloured brocades, provided with silk furniture of all sorts. Fill the tent afterwards with a variety of different perfumes, amber, musk, and all sorts of scents. Then fix the hangings so that nothing of these perfumes can escape out of the tent. Then, when you find the vapour strong enough to impregnate water, sit down on your throne, and send for the prophetess to come and see you in the tent. When you are thus together there, and she inhales the perfumes, she will delight in the same, all her bones will be relaxed in a soft repose, and finally she will be swooning. When you see her thus far gone, ask her to grant you her favours; she will not hesitate to accord them. Having once possessed her, you will be freed of the embarrassment caused to you by her and her *goum.'*

Moçailama had everything arranged accordingly.

When he saw that the perfumed vapour was dense enough to impregnate the water in the tent he sat down upon his throne and sent for the prophetess. On her arrival he gave orders to admit her into the tent; she entered and remained alone with him. He engaged her in conversation.

While Moçailama spoke to her she lost all her presence of mind, and became embarrassed and confused.

When he saw her in that state he knew that she desired cohabitation and he said: 'Come, rise and let me have possession of you; this place has been prepared for that purpose. If you like you may lie on your back, or you can place yourself on all fours, or kneel as in prayer, with your brow touching the ground, and your crupper in the air, forming a tripod. Whichever position you prefer, speak, and you shall be satisfied.'

The prophetess answered, 'I want it done in all ways. Let the revelation of God descend upon me, O Prophet of the Almighty.'

He at once precipitated himself upon her, and enjoyed her as he liked. She then said to him, 'When I am gone from here, ask my *goum* to give me to you in marriage.'

When she had left the tent and met her disciples, they said to her, 'What is the result of the conference, O prophetess of God?' and she replied, 'Moçailama has shown me what has been revealed to him, and I found it to be the truth, so obey him.'

Then Moçailama asked her in marriage from the *goum,* which was accorded to him. When the *goum* asked about the marriage-dowry of his future wife, he told them, 'I dispense you from saying the prayer *"aceur"* ' (which is said at three or four o'clock). Ever from that time the Beni-Temim do not pray at that hour; and when they are asked the reason, they answer, 'It is on account of our prophetess; she only knows the way to the truth.'

13

The man who deserves favours is, in the eyes of women, the one who is anxious to please them. He must be of good presence, excel in beauty those around him, be of good shape and well-formed proportions; true and sincere in his speech with women; he must likewise be generous and brave, not vainglorious, and pleasant in conversation. A slave to his promise, he must always keep his word, ever speak the truth, and do what he has said.

The man who boasts of his relations with women, of their acquaintance and good will to him, is a dastard. He will be spoken of in the next chapter.

There is a story that once there lived a king named Mamoum, who had a court fool of the name of Bahloul.

One day this buffoon appeared before the King. The King bade him to sit down, and then asked him, 'Why hast thou come, O son of a bad woman?'

Bahloul answered, 'I have come to see what has come to our Lord, whom may God make victorious.'

'And what has come to thee?' replied the King, 'and how art thou getting on with thy new and with thy old wife?' For Bahloul, not content with one wife, had married a second one.

'I am not happy,' he answered, 'neither with the old one, nor with the new one; and moreover poverty over-powers me.'

The King said, 'Can you recite any verses on this subject?'

'Certainly,' said Bahloul.

> By reason of my ignorance I have married two wives—
> And why do you complain, O husband of two wives?
> I said to myself, I shall be like a lamb between them;
> I shall take my pleasure upon the bosoms of my two sheep,
> And I have become like a ram between two female jackals,
> Days follow upon days, and nights upon nights,
> And their yoke bears me down during both days and nights.
> If I am kind to one, the other gets vexed.
> And so I cannot escape from these two furies.
> If you want to live well and with a free heart,
> And with your hands unclenched, then do not marry.
> If you must wed, then marry one wife only:
> One alone is enough to satisfy two armies.

When Mamoum heard these words he began to laugh, till he nearly tumbled over. Then, as a proof of his kindness, he gave to Bahloul his golden robe, a most beautiful vestment.

Bahloul went in high spirits towards the dwelling of the Grand Vizir. Just then Hamdonna looked from the height of her palace in that direction, and saw him. She said to her negress, 'By the

God of the temple of Mecca! There is Bahloul dressed in a fine gold-worked robe! How can I manage to get possession of the same?'

'Bahloul is a sly man,' replied the negress. 'People think generally that they can make fun of him; but, for God, it is he who makes fun of them. Give up the idea, mistress mine, and take care that you do not fall into the snare which you intend setting for him.'

But Hamdonna said again, 'It must be done!' She then sent her negress to Bahloul, to tell him that he should come to her.

Hamdonna welcomed him and said: 'Oh, Bahloul, I believe you come to hear me sing.' He replied: 'Most certainly, oh, my mistress! You have a marvellous gift for singing.'

'I also think that after having listened to my songs, you will be pleased to take some refreshments.'

'Yes,' said he.

Then she began to sing admirably, so as to make people who listened die with love.

After Bahloul had heard her sing, refreshments were served. Then she said to him: 'I do not know why, but I fancy you would gladly take off your robe, to make me a present of it.' And Bahloul answered: 'Oh, my mistress! I have sworn to give it to her to whom I have done as a man does to a woman.'

'Do you know what that is, Bahloul?' said she.

'Do I know it?' replied he. 'I, who am instructing God's creatures in that science? It is I who make them copulate in love, who initiate them in the delights a female can give, show them how one must caress a woman, and what will excite and satisfy her. Oh, my mistress, who should know the art of coition if it is not I?'

Hamdonna was the daughter of Mamoum, and the wife of the Grand Vizir. She was endowed with the most perfect beauty; of a superb figure and harmonious form. No one in her time surpassed her in grace and perfection. Heroes on seeing her became humble and submissive, and looked down to the ground for fear of temptation, so many charms and perfections had God lavished on her. Those who looked steadily at her were troubled in their mind, and oh! how many heroes imperilled themselves for her sake. For this very reason Bahloul had always avoided meeting her for fear of succumbing to the temptation; and, apprehensive for his peace of mind, had never, until then, been in her presence.

Bahloul began to converse with her. Now he looked at her and anon bent his eyes to the ground, fearful of not being able to command his passion. Hamdonna burnt with desire to have the robe, and he would not give it up without being paid for it.

15

'What price do you demand,' she asked. To which he replied, 'Coition, O apple of my eye.'

'You know what that is, O Bahloul?' said she.

'By God,' he cried; 'no man knows women better than I; they are the occupation of my life. No one has studied all their concerns more than I. I know what they are fond of; for learn, oh, lady mine, that men choose different occupations according to their genius and their bent. The one takes, the other gives; this one sells, the other buys. My only thought is of love and of the possession of beautiful women. I heal those that are lovesick, and carry a solace to their thirsting vaginas.'

Hamdonna was surprised at his words and the sweetness of his language. 'Could you recite me some verses on this subject?' she asked.

'Certainly,' he answered.

My whole ambition is in love and coition with women,
No doubt nor mistake about that!
If my member is without vulva, my state becomes frightful,
My heart then burns with a fire which cannot be quenched.
Look at my member erect! There it is—admire its beauty!
It calms the heat of love and quenches the hottest fires
By its movement in and out between your thighs.
Oh, my hope and my apple, oh, noble and generous lady,
If one time will not suffice to appease thy fire,
I shall do it again, so as to give satisfaction;
No one may reproach thee, for all the world does the same.
Let me come to you and do not repel me.
Let me come to you like one that brings drink to the thirsty;
Hasten and let my hungry eyes look at thy bosom.
Do not withhold from me love's joys, and do not be bashful,
Give yourself up to me—I shall never cause you trouble,
Even were you to fill me with sickness from head to foot.
I shall always remain as I am, and you as you are,
Knowing that I am the servant, and you are the mistress ever.
Then shall our love be veiled? It shall be hidden for all time,
For I keep it a secret and I shall be mute and muzzled.
It is by God's will that everything happens,
And he has filled me with love; but today my luck is ill.

While Hamdonna was listening she nearly swooned, and set herself to examine the member of Bahloul, which stood erect like a column between his thighs. Now she said to herself: 'I shall give myself up to him,' and now, 'No I will not.' During this uncertainty she felt a yearning for pleasure deep within her parts

16

privy; and Eblis made flow from her natural parts a moisture, the fore-runner of pleasure. She then no longer combated her desire to cohabit with him, and reassured herself by the thought: 'If this Bahloul, after having had his pleasure with me, should divulge it no one will believe his words.'

She requested him to divest himself of his robe and to come into her room, but Bahloul replied: 'I shall not undress till I have sated my desire, O apple of my eye.'

Then Hamdonna rose, trembling with excitement for what was to follow; she undid her girdle, and left the room, Bahloul following her and thinking: 'Am I really awake or is this a dream?' He walked after her till she had entered her boudoir. Then she threw herself on a couch of silk, which was rounded on the top like a vault, lifted her clothes up over her thighs, trembling all over, and all the beauty which God had given her was in Bahloul's arms.

Bahloul examined the belly of Hamdonna, round like an elegant cupola, his eyes dwelt upon a navel which was like a pearl in a golden cup; and descending lower down there was a beautiful piece of nature's workmanship, and the whiteness and shape of her thighs surprised him.

Then he pressed Hamdonna in a passionate embrace, and soon saw the animation leave her face; she seemed almost unconscious. She had lost her head; and holding Bahloul's member in her hands, excited and fired him more and more.

Bahloul said to her: 'Why do I see you so troubled and beside yourself?' And she answered: 'Leave me, O son of a debauched woman! By God, I am like a mare in heat, and you continue to excite me still more with your words, and what words! They would set any woman on fire, if she was the purest creature in the world. You will insist in making me succumb by your talk and your verses.'

Bahloul answered: 'Am I then not like your husband?' 'Yes,' she said, 'but a woman gets heat on account of the man, as a mare on account of the horse, whether the man be the husband or not; with this difference, however, that the mare gets lusty only at certain periods of the year, and only then receives the stallion, while a woman can always be made rampant by words of love. Both these dispositions have met within me, and, as my husband is absent, make haste, for he will soon be back.'

Bahloul replied: 'Oh, my mistress, my loins hurt me and prevent me mounting upon you. You take the man's position, and then take my robe and let me depart.'

Then he laid himself down in the position the woman takes

in receiving a man; and his verge was standing up like a column.

Hamdonna threw herself upon Bahloul, took his member between her hands and began to look at it. She was astonished at its size, strength and firmness, and cried: 'Here we have the ruin of all women and the cause of many troubles. O Bahloul! I never saw a more beautiful dart than yours!' Still she continued keeping hold of it, and rubbed its head against the lips of her vulva till the latter part seemed to say: 'O member, come into me.'

Then Bahloul inserted his member into the vagina of the Sultan's daughter, and she, settling down upon his engine, allowed it to penetrate entirely into her furnace till nothing more could be seen of it, not the slightest trace, and she said: 'How lascivious has God made woman, and how indefatigable after her pleasures.' She then gave herself up to an up-and-down dance, moving her bottom like a riddle; to the right and left, and forward and backward; never was there such a dance as this.

The Sultan's daughter continued her ride upon Bahloul's member till the moment of enjoyment arrived, and the attraction of the vulva seemed to pump the member as though by suction: just as an infant sucks the teat of the mother. The acme of enjoyment came to both simultaneously, and each took the pleasure with avidity.

Then Hamdonna seized the member in order to with-draw it, and slowly, slowly she made it come out, saying: 'This is the deed of a vigorous man.' Then she dried it and her own private parts with a silken kerchief, and rose.

Bahloul also got up and prepared to depart, but she said, 'And the robe?'

He answered, 'Why, O mistress! You have been riding me, and still want a present?'

'But,' said she, 'did you not tell me that you could not mount me on account of the pains in your loins?'

'It matters but little,' said Bahloul. 'The first time it was your turn, the second will be mine, and the price for it will be the robe, and then I will go.'

Hamdonna thought to herself, 'As he began he may now go on; afterwards he will go away.'

So she laid herself down, but Bahloul said, 'I shall not lie with you unless you undress entirely.'

Then she undressed until she was quite naked, and Bahloul fell into an ecstasy on seeing the beauty and perfection of her form. He looked at her magnificent thighs and rebounding navel, at her belly vaulted like an arch, her plump breasts standing out like hyacinths. Her neck was like a gazelle's, the opening of her mouth like a ring, her lips fresh and red like a gory sabre. Her teeth might have been taken for pearls and her cheeks for roses. Her eyes were black and well slit, and her eyebrows of ebony resembled the rounded flourish of the *noun* traced by the hand of a skilful writer. Her forehead was like the full moon in the night.

Bahloul began to embrace her, to suck her lips and to kiss her bosom; he drew her fresh saliva and bit her thighs. So he went on till she was ready to swoon, and could scarcely stammer, and her eyes became veiled. Then he kissed her vulva, and she moved neither hand nor foot. He looked lovingly upon the secret parts of Hamdonna, beautiful enough to attract all eyes with their purple centre.

Bahloul cried, 'Oh, the temptation of man!' and still he bit her and kissed her till her desire was roused to its full pitch. Her sighs came quicker, and grasping his member with her hand she made it disappear in her vagina.

Then it was he who moved hard, and she who responded hotly, the overwhelming pleasure simultaneously calming their fervour.

Then Bahloul got off her, dried his pestle and her mortar, and prepared to retire. But Hamdonna said, 'Where is the robe? You mock me, O Bahloul.' He answered, 'O my mistress, I shall only part with it for a consideration. You have had your dues and I mine. The first time was for you, the second time for me; now the third time shall be for the robe.'

This said, he took it off, folded it, and put it in Hamdonna's hands, who, having risen, laid down again on the couch and said, 'Do what you like!'

Forthwith Bahloul threw himself upon her, and with one push completely buried his member in her vagina; then he began to work as with a pestle, and she to move her bottom, until both again did flow over at the same time. Then he rose from her side, left his robe, and went.

The negress said to Hamdonna, 'O my mistress, is it not as I have told you? Bahloul is a bad man, and you could not get the better of him. They consider him as a subject for mockery, but, before God, he is making fun of them. Why would you not believe me?'

Hamdonna turned to her and said, 'Do not tire me with your remarks. It came to pass what had to come to pass, and on the opening of each vulva is inscribed the name of the man who is to enter it, right or wrong, for love or for hatred. If Bahloul's name had not been inscribed on my vulva he would never have got into it, had he offered me the universe with all it contains.'

As they were thus talking there came a knock at the door. The negress asked who was there, and in answer the voice of Bahloul said, 'It is I.' Hamdonna, in doubt as to what the buffoon wanted to do, got frightened. The negress asked Bahloul what he wanted, and received the reply, 'Bring me a little water.' She went out of the house with a cup full of water. Bahloul drank, and then let the cup slip out of his hands, and it was broken. The negress shut the door upon Bahloul, who sat himself down on the threshold.

The buffoon being thus close to the door, the Vizir, Hamdonna's husband, arrived, who said to him, 'Why do I see you here, O Bahloul?' And he answered, 'O my lord, I was passing through this street when I was overcome by a great thirst. A negress came and brought me a cup of water. The cup slipped from my hands and got broken. Then our lady Hamdonna took my robe, which the Sultan our Master had given me as indemnification.'

Then said the Vizir, 'Let him have his robe.' Hamdonna at this moment came out, and her husband asked her whether it was true that she had taken the robe in payment for the cup. Hamdonna then cried, beating her hands together, 'What have you done, O Bahloul?' He answered, 'I have talked to your husband the language of my folly; talk to him, you, the language of thy wisdom.' And she, enraptured with the cunning he had displayed, gave him back his robe, and he departed.

CHAPTER 2

Concerning Women who Deserve to be Praised

Know, o Vizir (and the mercy of God be with you!) that there
are women of all sorts; that there are such as are worthy of
praise, and such as deserve nothing but contempt.

In order that a woman may be relished by men, she must
have a perfect waist, and must be plump and lusty. Her hair will
be black, her forehead wide, she will have eyebrows of Ethiopian
blackness, large black eyes, with the whites in them very limpid.
With cheek of perfect oval, she will have an elegant nose and a
graceful mouth; lips and tongue vermilion; her breath will be
of pleasant odour, her throat long, her neck strong, her bust and
her belly large; her breasts must be full and firm, her belly in good
proportion, and her navel well-developed and marked; the lower
part of the belly is to be large, the vulva projecting and fleshy,
from the point where the hairs grow, to the buttocks; the conduit
must be narrow and not moist, soft to the touch, and emitting a
strong heat and no bad smell; she must have the thighs and
buttocks hard, the hips large and full, a waist of fine shape,
hands and feet of striking elegance, plump arms, and well-
developed shoulders.

If one looks at a woman with those qualities in front, one is
fascinated; if from behind, one dies with pleasure. Looked at
sitting, she is a rounded dome; lying, a soft-bed; standing, the
staff of a standard. When she is walking, her natural parts
appear as set off under her clothing. She speaks and laughs
rarely, and never without a reason. She never leaves the house,
even to see neighbours of her acquaintance. She has no women
friends, gives her confidence to nobody, and her husband is her
sole reliance. She takes nothing from anyone, excepting from her
husband and her parents. If she sees relatives, she does not
meddle with their affairs. She is not treacherous, and has no
faults to hide, nor bad reasons to proffer. She does not try to
entice people. If her husband shows his intention of performing
the conjugal rite, she is agreeable to his desires and occasionally
even provokes them. She assists him always in his affairs, and is

21

sparing in complaints and tears; she does not laugh or rejoice when she sees her husband moody or sorrowful, but shares his troubles, and wheedles him into good humour, till he is quite content again. She does not surrender herself to anybody but her husband, even if abstinence would kill her. She hides her secret parts, and does not allow them to be seen; she is always elegantly attired, of the utmost personal propriety, and takes care not to let her husband see what might be repugnant to him. She perfumes herself with scents, uses antimony for her toilets, and cleans her teeth with *souak*.

Such a woman is cherished by all men.

The Story of the Negro Dorérame

The story goes, and God knows its truth, that there was once a powerful King who had a large kingdom, armies and allies. His name was Ali ben Direme.

One night, not being able to sleep at all, he called his Vizir, the Chief of the Police, and the Commander of his Guards.

He told them: 'Sleep will not come to me; I wish to walk through the town tonight, and I must have you ready at my hand during my round.'

'To hear is to obey,' they replied.

The King then left, saying: 'In the name of God! and may the blessing of the Prophet be with us.'

His suite followed, and accompanied him everywhere.

So they went on, until they heard a noise in one of the streets, and saw a man in the most violent passion stretched on the ground, face downwards, beating his breast with a stone and crying, 'Ah there is no longer any justice here below! Is there nobody who will tell the King what is going on in his states?' And he repeated incessantly: 'There is no longer any justice! she has disappeared and the whole world is in mourning.'

The King said to his attendants, 'Bring this man to me quietly, and be careful not to frighten him.' They went to him, took him by the hand, and said to him, 'Rise and have no fear—no harm will come to you.'

The King then asked him, 'What mean these words I have heard: "Ah! there is no more justice here below! Nobody tells the King what is going on in his states!" Tell me what has happened to you.'

'What I shall now tell you,' said the man, 'is marvellous and surprising. I loved a woman, who loved me also, and we were united in love. These relations lasted a long while, until an old

22

woman enticed my mistress and took her away to a house of misfortune, shame and debauchery. Then sleep fled from my couch; I have lost all my happiness, and I have fallen into the abyss of misfortune.'

The King then said to him, 'Which is that house of ill omen, and with whom is the woman?'

The man replied, 'She is with a negro of the name of Dorérame, who has at his house women beautiful as the moon, the likes of whom the King has not in his place. He has a mistress who has a profound love for him, is entirely devoted to him, and who sends him all he wants in the way of silver, beverages and clothing.'

The King was much surprised at what he had heard, but the Vizir, who had not missed a word of this conversation, had certainly made out that the negro was no other than his own.

The King requested the man to show him the house.

'If I show it you, what will you do?' asked the man.

'You will see what I shall do,' said the King. 'You will not be able to do anything,' replied the man, 'for it is a place which must be respected and feared. If you want to enter it by force you will risk death, for its master is redoubtable by means of his strength and courage.'

'Show me the place,' said the King, 'and have no fear.' The man answered, 'So be it as God will!'

He then rose, and walked before them. They followed him to a wide street, where he stopped in front of a house with lofty doors, the walls being on all sides high and inaccessible.

They examined the walls, looking for a place where they might be scaled, but with no result. To their surprise they found the house to be as close as a breastplate.

The King, turning to the man, asked him, 'What is your name?'

'Omar ben Isad,' he replied.

Then the King, addressing his attendants said, 'Are you determined? Is there one amongst you who could scale these walls?'

'Impossible!' they all replied.

Then said the King, 'I myself will scale this wall, so please God on high! but by means of an expedient for which I require your assistance, and if you lend me the same I shall scale the wall, if it pleases God on high.'

They said, 'What is there to be done?'

'Tell me,' said the King, 'who is the strongest amongst you.' They replied, 'The Chief of the Police, who is your *Chaouch*.'

The King said, 'And who next?'

'The Commander of the Guards.'

'And after him, who?' asked the King.

'The Grand Vizir.'

Omar listened with astonishment. He knew now that it was the King, and his joy was great.

The King said, 'Who is there yet?'

Omar replied, 'I, O my master.'

The King said to him, 'O Omar, you have found out who we are; but do not betray our disguise, and you will be absolved from blame.'

'To hear is to obey,' said Omar.

The King then said to the *Chaouch*, 'Rest your hands against the wall so that your back projects.'

The *Chaouch* did so.

Then said the King to the commander of the guards, 'Mount upon the back of the *Chaouch*.' Then the King ordered the Vizir to mount.

Then said the King, 'O Omar, mount upon the highest place!' And Omar then got on to the shoulders of the *Chaouch*, and from there upon the back of the Commander of the Guards, and then upon that of the Vizir, and, standing upon the shoulders of the latter, he took the same position as the others.

Then the King said, 'In the name of God! and his blessing be with the prophet, upon whom be the mercy and salutation of God!' and, placing his hand upon the back of the *Chaouch*, he then did the same with the others, until he got upon Omar's back. Then, placing his feet upon Omar's shoulders, the King could with his hands grasp the terrace; he made a spring, and stood upon the terrace.

The King then began to look for a place for descending, but found no passage. He unrolled his turban, fixed one end with a single knot, and let himself down into the courtyard.

He then set himself to examine the place where he found himself, and counted the chambers one after another. He found seventeen chambers or rooms, furnished in different styles, with tapestries and velvet hangings of various colours, from the first to the last.

Examining all round, he saw a place raised by seven stair-steps, from which issued a great noise from voices. He went up to it, saying, 'O God! favour my project, and let me come safe and sound out of here.'

He then arrived at the curtain hanging at the entrance; it was of red brocade. From there he examined the room, which was bathed in light, filled with many chandeliers, and candles burning in golden sconces. In the middle of this saloon played a jet of musk-water. A table-cloth extended from end to end, covered with sundry meats and fruits.

The saloon was provided with gilt furniture, the splendour of which dazzled the eye. In fact, everywhere, there were ornaments of all kinds.

On looking closer the King ascertained that round the table-cloth there were twelve maidens and seven women, all like moons; he was astonished at their beauty and grace. There were likewise with them seven negroes, and this sight filled him with surprise. His attention was above all attracted by a woman like the full moon, of perfect beauty, with black eyes, oval cheeks, and a lithe and graceful waist; she humbled the hearts of those who became enamoured of her.

Stupefied by her beauty, the King was as one stunned. He then said to himself, 'How is there any getting out of this place? O my spirit, do not give way to love!'

And continuing his inspection of the room, he perceived in the hands of those who were present, glasses filled with wine. They were drinking and eating, and it was easy to see they were overcome with drink.

While the King was pondering how to escape his embarrassment, he heard one of the women saying to one of her companions, calling her by name, 'Oh, so and so, rise and light a torch, so that we can go to bed, for sleep is overpowering us. Come, light the torch, and let us retire to the other chamber.'

They rose and lifted up the curtain to leave the room. The King hid himself to let them pass; then, perceiving that they had left their chamber to do a thing necessary and obligatory in human kind, he took advantage of their absence, entered their apartment, and hid himself in a cupboard.

Whilst he was thus in hiding the women returned and shut the doors. Their reason was obscured by the fumes of wine; they pulled off all their clothes and began to caress each other mutually.

The King said to himself, 'Omar has told me true about this house of misfortune as an abyss of debauchery.'

When the women had fallen asleep the King rose, extinguished the light, undressed, and laid down between the two. He had taken care during their conversation to impress their names on his memory. So he was able to say to one of them, 'You, so and so, where have you put the door-keys?' speaking very low.

The woman answered, 'Go to sleep, you whore, the keys are in their usual place.'

The King said to himself, 'There is no might and strength but in God the Almighty and Benevolent!' and was much troubled.

And again he asked the woman about the keys, saying, 'Daylight is coming. I must open the doors. There is the sun. I am going to open the house.'

And she answered, 'The keys are in the usual place. Why do you thus bother me? Sleep, I say, till it is day.'

And again the King said to himself, 'There is no might and strength but in God the Almighty and Benevolent, and surely if it were not for the fear of God I should run my sword through her.' Then he began again, 'Oh, you, so and so!'

She said, 'What do you want?'

'I am uneasy,' said the King, 'about the keys; tell me where they are?'

And she answered, 'You hussy! Does your vulva itch for coition? Cannot you do without for a single night? Look! the Vizir's wife has withstood all the entreaties of the negro, and repelled him since six months! Go, the keys are in the negro's pocket. Do not say to him, "Give me the keys;" but say, "Give me your member." You know his name is Dorérame.'

The King was now silent, for he knew what to do. He waited a short time till the woman was asleep; then he dressed himself in her clothes, and concealed his sword under them; his face he hid under a veil of red silk. Thus dressed he looked like other women. Then he opened the door, stole softly out, and placed himself behind the curtains of the saloon entrance. He saw only some people sitting there; the remainder were asleep.

The King made the following silent prayer, 'O my soul, let me follow the right way, and let all those people among whom I find myself be stunned with drunkenness, so that they cannot know the King from his subjects, and God give me strength.'

He then entered the saloon saying: 'In the name of God!' and he tottered towards the bed of the negro as if drunk. The negroes and the women took him to be the woman whose attire he had taken.

Dorérame had a great desire to have his pleasure with that woman, and when he saw her sit down by the bed he thought that she had broken her sleep to come to him, perhaps for love games. So he said, 'Oh, you, so and so, undress and get into my bed, I shall soon be back.'

The King said to himself, 'There is no might and strength but in the High God, the Benevolent!' Then he searched for the keys in the clothes and pockets of the negro, but found nothing. He said, 'God's will be done!' Then raising his eyes, he saw a

26

high window; he reached up with his arm, and found gold embroidered garments there; he slipped his hands into the pockets, and, oh, surprise! he found the keys. He examined them and counted seven, corresponding to the number of the doors of the house, and in his joy, he exclaimed, 'God, be praised and glorified!' Then he said, 'I can only get out of here by a ruse.' Then feigning sickness, and appearing as if he wanted to vomit violently, he held his hand before his mouth, and hurried to the centre of the courtyard. The negro said to him, 'God bless you! oh, so and so! any other woman would have been sick into the bed!'

The King then went to the inner door of the house, and opened it; he closed it behind him, and so from one door to the other, till he came to the seventh, which opened upon the street. Here he found his companions again, who had been in great anxiety, and who asked him what he had seen?

Then said the King: 'This is not the time to answer. Let us go into this house with the blessing of God and with his help.'

They resolved to be upon their guard, there being in the house seven negroes, twelve maidens, and seven women, beautiful as moons.

The Vizir asked the King, 'What garments are these?' And the King answered, 'Be silent; without them I should never have got the keys.'

He then went to the chamber where were the two women, with whom he had been lying, took off the clothes in which he was dressed, and resumed his own, taking good care of his sword. Repairing to the saloon, where the negroes and the women were, he and his companions ranged themselves behind the door-curtain.

After having looked into the saloon, they said, 'Amongst all these women there is none more beautiful than the one seated on the elevated cushion!' The King said, 'I reserve her for myself, if she does not belong to someone else.'

While they were examining the interior of the saloon, Dorérame descended from the bed, and after him one of those beautiful women. Then another negro got on the bed with another woman, and so on till the seventh. They rode them in this way, one after the other, excepting the beautiful woman mentioned above, and the maidens. Each of these women appeared to mount upon the bed with marked reluctance, and descended, after the coition was finished, with her head bent down.

The negroes, however, were lusting after, and pressing one after the other, the beautiful woman. But she spurned them all, saying, 'I shall never consent to it, and as to these virgins, I take them also under my protection.'

Dorérame then rose and went up to her, holding in his hands his member in full erection, stiff as a pillar. He hit her with it on the face and head, saying, 'Six times this night I have pressed you to cede to my desires, and you always refuse; but now I must have you, even this night.'

When the woman saw the stubbornness of the negro and the state of drunkenness he was in, she tried to soften him by promises. 'Sit down here by me,' she said, 'and tonight thy desires shall be contented.'

The negro sat down near to her with his member still erect as a column. The King could scarcely master his surprise.

Then the woman began to sing the following verses, intoning them from the bottom of her heart:

I prefer a young man for coition, and him only;
He is full of courage—he is my sole ambition,
His member is strong to deflower the virgin,
And richly proportioned in all its dimensions;
It has a head like to a brazier.
Enormous, and none like it in creation;
Strong it is and hard, with the head rounded off.
It is always ready for action and does not die down;
It never sleeps, owing to the violence of its love.
It sighs to enter my vulva, and sheds tears on my belly;
It asks not for help, not being in want of any;
It has no need of an ally, and stands alone the greatest fatigues,
And nobody can be sure of what will result from its efforts.
Full of vigour and life, it bores into my vagina,
And it works about there in action constant and splendid.
First from the front to the back, and then from the right to the left;
Now it is crammed hard in by vigorous pressure,
Now it rubs its head on the orifice of my vagina.
And he strokes my back, my stomach, my sides,
Kisses my cheeks, and anon begins to suck at my lips.
He embraces me close, and makes me roll on the bed,
And between his arms I am like a corpse without life.
Every part of my body receives in turn his love-bites,
And he covers me with kisses of fire;
When he sees me in heat he quickly comes to me,
Then he opens my thighs and kisses my belly,
And puts his tool in my hand to make it knock at my door.
Soon he is in the cave, and I feel pleasure approaching.

He shakes me and trills me, and hotly we both are working,
And he says, 'Receive my seed!' and I answer, 'Oh give it beloved
  one!
It shall be welcome to me, you light of my eyes!
Oh, you man of all men, who fillest me with pleasure.
Oh, you soul of my soul, go on with fresh vigour,
For you must not yet withdraw it from me; leave it there,
And this day will then be free of all sorrow.'
He has sworn to God to have me for seventy nights,
And what he wished for he did, in the way of kisses and embraces,
  during all those nights.

When she had finished, the King, in great surprise, said, 'How lascivious has God made this woman.' And turning to his companions, 'There is no doubt that this woman has no husband, and has not been debauched, for, certainly that negro is in love with her, and she has nevertheless repulsed him.'

Omar ben Isad took the word, 'This is true, O King! Her husband has been now away for nearly a year, and many men have endeavoured to debauch her, but she has resisted.'

The King asked, 'Who is her husband?' And his companions answered, 'She is the wife of the son of your father's Vizir.'

The King replied, 'You speak true; I have indeed heard it said that the son of my father's Vizir had a wife without fault, endowed with beauty and perfection and of exquisite shape; not adulterous and innocent of debauchery.'

'This is the same woman,' said they.

The King said, 'No matter how, but I must have her,' and turning to Omar, he added, 'Where, amongst these women, is your mistress?' Omar answered, 'I do not see her, O King!' Upon which the King said, 'Have patience, I will show her to you.' Omar was quite surprised to find that the King knew so much. 'And this then is the negro Dorérame?' asked the King. 'Yes, and he is a slave of mine,' answered the Vizir. 'Be silent, this is not the time to speak,' said the King.

While this discourse was going on, the negro Dorérame, still desirous of obtaining the favours of that lady, said to her, 'I am tired of your lies, O Beder el Bedour' (full moon of the full moons), for so she called herself.

The King said, 'He who called her so called her by her true name, for she is the full moon of the full moons, afore God!'

However, the negro wanted to draw the woman away with him, and hit her in the face.

The King, mad with jealousy, and with his heart full of ire, said to the Vizir, 'Look what your negro is doing! By God! he shall die the death of a villain, and I shall make an example of him, and a warning to those who would imitate him!'

At that moment the King heard the lady say to the negro, 'You are betraying your master the Vizir with his wife, and now you betray her, in spite of your intimacy with her and the favours she grants to you. And surely she loves you passionately, and you are pursuing another woman!'

The King said to the Vizir, 'Listen, and do not speak a word.'

The lady then rose and returned to the place where she had been before, and began to recite:

Oh, men! listen to what I say on the subject of woman,
Her thirst for coition is written between her eyes.
Do not put trust in her vows, even were she the Sultan's daughter.
Woman's malice is boundless; not even the King of kings
Would suffice to subdue it, whate'er be his might.
Men, take heed and shun the love of woman!
Do not say, 'Such a one is my well beloved;'
Do not say, 'She is my life's companion.'
If I deceive you, then say my words are untruths.
As long as she is with you in bed, you have her love,
But a woman's love is not enduring, believe me.
Lying upon her breast, you are her love-treasure;
Whilst the coition goes on, you have her love, poor fool!
But, anon, she looks upon you as a fiend;
And this is a fact undoubted and certain.
The wife receives the slave in the bed of the master,
And the serving-men allay upon her their lust.
Certain it is, such conduct is not to be praised and honoured.
But the virtue of women is frail and changeful,
And the man thus deceived is looked upon with contempt.
Therefore a man with a heart should not put trust in a woman.

At these words the Vizir began to cry, but the King bade him to be quiet. Then the negro recited the following verses in response to those of the lady:

Oh, you women all! for sure you have no patience when the virile
*   member you are wanting,*
For in the same resides your life and death;
It is the end and all of your wishes, secret or open.
If your choler and ire are aroused against your husbands,
They appease you simply by introducing their members.

Your religion resides in your vulva, and the manly member is your soul.
Such you will always find is the nature of woman.

With that, the negro threw himself upon the woman, who pushed him back.

At this moment, the King felt his heart oppressed; he drew his sword, as did his companions, and they entered the room. The negroes and women saw nothing but brandished swords.

One of the negroes rose, and rushed upon the King and his companions, but the *Chaouch* severed with one blow his head from his body. The King cried, 'God's blessing upon you! Your arm is not withered and your mother has not borne a weakling. You have struck down your enemies, and paradise shall be your dwelling and place of rest!'

Another negro got up and aimed a blow at the *Chaouch,* which broke the sword of the *Chaouch* in twain. It had been a beautiful weapon, and the *Chaouch,* on seeing it ruined, broke out into the most violent passion; he seized the negro by the arm, lifted him up, and threw him against the wall, breaking his bones. Then the King cried, 'God is great. He has not dried up your hand. Oh, what a *Chaouch*! God grant you his blessing.'

The negroes, when they saw this, were cowed and silent, and the King, master of their lives, said, 'The man that lifts his hand only, shall lose his head!' And he commanded that the remaining five negroes should have their hands tied behind their backs.

This having been done, he turned to Beder el Bedour and asked her, 'Whose wife are you, and who is this negro?'

She then told him on that subject what he had heard already from Omar. And the King thanked her, saying, 'May God give you his blessing.' He then asked her, 'How long can a woman patiently do without coition?' She seemed amazed, but the King said, 'Speak, and do not be abashed.'

She then answered, 'A well-born lady of high origin can remain for six months without; but a lowly woman of no race nor high blood, who does not respect herself when she can lay her hand upon a man, will have him upon her; his stomach and his member will know her vagina.'

Then said the King, pointing to one of the women, 'Who is this one?' She answered, 'This is the wife of the *Kadi.*' 'And this one?' 'The wife of the second Vizir.' 'And this?' 'The wife of the chief of the *Muftis.*' 'And that one?' 'The Treasurer's.' 'And

those two women that are in the other room?' She answe
'They have received the hospitality of the house, and one
them was brought here yesterday by an old woman; the neg
has so far not got possession of her.'

Then said Omar, 'This is the one I spoke to you about, O my
master.'

'And the other woman? To whom does she belong?' said the
King.

'She is the wife of the *Amine* of the carpenters,' answered
she.

Then said the King, 'And these girls, who are they?'

She answered, 'This one is the daughter of the clerk of the
treasury; this other one the daughter of the *Mohtesib,* the third
is the daughter of the *Bouab,* the next one the daughter of the
Amine of the *Moueddin;* that one the daughter of the colour-
keeper. At the invitation of the King, she passed them thus
all in review.

The King then asked for the reason of so many women being
brought together there.

Beder el Bedour replied, 'O master of ours, the negro knows
no other passions than for coition and good wine. He keeps
making love night and day, and his member rests only when he
himself is asleep.'

She said, 'Upon yolks of eggs fried in fat and swimming in
honey, and upon white bread; he drinks nothing but old muscatel
wine.'

The King said, 'Who has brought these women here, who, all
of them, belong to officials of the State?'

She replied, 'O master of ours, he has in his service an old
woman who has had the run of the houses in the town; she
chooses and brings to him any woman of superior beauty and
perfection; but she serves him only against good consideration
in silver, dresses, etc., precious stones, rubies, and other objects
of value.'

'And whence does the negro get that silver?' asked the King.
The lady remaining silent, he added, 'Give me some information,
please.'

She signified with a sign from the corner of her eye that he
had got it all from the wife of the Grand Vizir.

The King understood her, and continued, 'O Beder el Bedour!
I have faith and confidence in you, and your testimony will have
in my eyes the value of that of the two *Adels.* Speak to me
without reserve as to what concerns yourself.'

She answered him, 'I have not been touched, and however

...ing this might have lasted the negro would not have had his desire satisfied.'

'Is this so?' asked the King.

She replied, 'It is so!' She had understood what the King wanted to say, and the King had seized the meaning of her words.

The King having asked her then who those negroes were, she answered, 'They are his companions. After he had quite surfeited himself with the women he had caused to be brought to him, he handed them over to them, as you have seen. If it were not for the protection of a woman where would that man be?'

Then spoke the King, 'O Beder el Bedour, why did not your husband ask my help against this oppression? Why did you not complain?'

She replied, 'O King of the time, O beloved Sultan, O master of numerous armies and allies! As regards my husband I was so far unable to inform him of my lot; as to myself I have nothing to say but what you know by the verses I sang just now. I have given advice to men about women from the first verse to the last.'

The King said, 'O Beder el Bedour! I like you, I have put the question to you in the name of the chosen Prophet (the benediction and mercy of God be with him!). Inform me of everything; you have nothing to fear; I give you the *aman* complete. Has this negro not enjoyed you? For I presume that none of you were out of reach of his attempts and had her honour safe.'

She replied, 'O King of our time, in the name of your high rank and your power! Look! He, about whom you ask me, I would not have accepted him as a legitimate husband; how could I have consented to grant him the favour of an illicit love?'

The King said, 'You appear to be sincere, but the verses I heard you sing have roused doubts in my soul.'

She replied, 'I had three motives for employing that language. Firstly, I was at that moment in heat, like a young mare; secondly, Eblis had excited my natural parts; and lastly, I wanted to quiet the negro and make him have patience, so that he should grant me some delay and leave me in peace until God would deliver me of him.'

The King said, 'Do you speak seriously?' She was silent. Then the King cried, 'O Beder el Bedour, you alone shall be pardoned!' She understood that it was she only that the King would spare from the punishment of death. He then cautioned her that she must keep the secret, and said he wanted to leave now.

Then all the women and virgins approached Beder el Bedour and implored her, saying, 'Intercede for us, for you have power over the King;' and they shed tears over her hands, and in despair threw themselves down.

Beder el Bedour then called the King back, as he was going, and said to him, 'O our master! you have not granted me any favour yet.' 'How,' said he, 'I have sent for a beautiful mule for you; you will mount her and come with us. As for these women, they must all of them die.'

She then said, 'O our master! I ask you and conjure you to authorise me to make a stipulation which you will accept.' The King made oath that he would fulfil it. Then she said, 'I ask as a gift the pardon of all these women and of all these maidens. Their deaths would moreover throw the most terrible consternation over the whole town.'

The King said, 'There is no might nor power but in God, the merciful!' He then ordered the negroes to be taken out and beheaded. The only exception he made was with the negro Dorérame, who was enormously stout and had a neck like a bull. They cut off his ears, nose, and lips; likewise his virile member, which they put into his mouth, and then hung him on a gallows.

Then the King ordered the seven doors of the house to be closed, and returned to his palace.

At sunrise he sent a mule to Beder el Bedour, in order to let her be brought to him. He made her dwell with him, and found her to be excelling all those who excel.

Then the King caused the wife of Omar ben Isad to be restored to him, and he made him his private secretary. After which he ordered the Vizir to repudiate his wife. He did not forget the *Chaouch* and the Commander of the Guards, to whom he made large presents, as he had promised, using for that purpose the negro's hoards. He sent the son of his father's Vizir to prison. He also caused the old go-between to be brought before him, and asked her, 'Give me all the particulars about the conduct of the negro, and tell me whether it was well done to bring in that way women to men.' She answered, 'This is the trade of nearly all old women.' He then had her executed, as well as all old women who followed that trade, and thus cut off in his State the tree of panderism at the root, and burnt the trunk.

He besides sent back to their families all the women and girls, and bade them repent in the name of God.

This story presents but a small part of the tricks and stratagems used by women against their husbands.

The moral of the tale is, that a man who falls in love with a woman imperils himself, and exposes himself to the greatest troubles.

CHAPTER 3

About Men who are to be Held in Contempt

Know, o my brother (to whom God be merciful), that a man who is misshapen, of coarse appearance, and whose member is short, thin and flabby, is contemptible in the eyes of women.

When such a man has a bout with a woman, he does not do his business with vigour and in a manner to give her enjoyment. He lays himself down upon her without previous toying, he does not kiss her, nor twine himself round her; he does not bite her, nor suck her lips, nor tickle her.

He gets upon her before she has begun to long for pleasure, and then he introduces with infinite trouble a member soft and nerveless. Scarcely has he commenced when he is already done for; he makes one or two movements, and then sinks upon the woman's breast to spend his sperm; and that is the most he can do. This done he with-draws his affair, and makes all haste to get down again from her.

Such a man—as was said by a writer—is quick in ejaculation and slow as to erection; after the trembling, which follows the ejaculation of the seed, his chest is heavy and his sides ache.

Qualities like these are no recommendation with women. Despicable also is the man who is false in his words; who does not fulfil the promise he has made; who never speaks without telling lies, and who conceals from his wife all his doings, except the adulterous exploits which he commits.

Women cannot esteem such men, as they cannot procure them any enjoyment.

It is said that a man of the name of Abbés, whose member was extremely small and slight, had a very corpulent wife, whom he could not contrive to satisfy in coition, so that she soon began to complain to her female friends about it.

This woman possessed a considerable fortune, whilst Abbés was very poor; and when he wanted anything, she was sure not to let him have what he wanted.

One day he went to see a wise man, and submitted his case to him.

The sage told him: 'If you had a fine member you might dispose of her fortune. Do you not know that women's religion is in their vulvas? But I will prescribe you a remedy which will do away with your troubles.'

Abbés lost no time in making up the remedy according to the recipe of the wise man, and after he had used it his member grew to be long and thick. When his wife saw it in that state she was surprised; but it was still better when he made her feel in the matter of enjoyment quite another thing than she had been accustomed to experience; he began in fact to work her with his tool in quite a remarkable manner, to such a point that she trembled and sighed and sobbed and cried out during the operation.

As soon as the wife found in her husband such eminently good qualities she gave him her fortune, and placed her person and all she had at his disposal.

CHAPTER 4

About Women who are to be Held in Contempt

Know, o Vizir (to whom God be merciful), that women differ in their natural dispositions: there are women who are worthy of all praise; and there are, on the other hand, women who only merit contempt.

The woman who merits the contempt of men is ugly and garrulous; her hair is woolly, her forehead projecting, her eyes are small and blear, her nose is enormous, the lips lead-coloured, the mouth large, the cheeks wrinkled and she shows gaps in her teeth; her cheekbones shine purple, and she sports bristles on her chin; her head sits on a meagre neck, with very much developed tendons; her shoulders are contracted and her chest is narrow, with flabby pendulous breasts, and her belly is like an empty leather-bottle, with the navel standing out like a heap of stones; her flanks are shaped like arcades; the bones of her spinal column may be counted; there is no flesh upon her croup; her vulva is large and cold.

Finally, such a woman has large knees and feet, big hands and emaciated legs.

A woman with such blemishes can give no pleasure to men in general, and least of all to him who is her husband or who enjoys her favours.

The man who approaches a woman like that with his member in erection will find it presently soft and relaxed, as though he was only close to a beast of burden. May God keep us from a woman of that description!

Contemptible likewise is the woman who is constantly laughing out; for, as it was said by an author, 'If you see a woman who is always laughing, fond of gaming and jesting, always running to her neighbours, meddling with matters that are no concern of hers, plaguing her husband with constant complaints, leaguing herself with other women against him, playing the grand lady, accepting gifts from everybody, know that that woman is a whore without shame.'

And again to be despised is the woman of a sombre, frowning nature, and one who is prolific in talk; the woman who is light-headed in her relations with men, or contentious, or fond of tittle-tattle and unable to keep her husband's secrets, or who is malicious. The woman of a malicious nature talks only to tell lies; if she makes a promise she does so only to break it, and if anybody confides in her, she betrays him; she is debauched, thievish, a scold, coarse and violent; she cannot give good advice; she is always occupied with the affairs of other people, and with such as bring harm, and is always on the watch for frivolous news; she is fond of repose, but not of work; she uses unbecoming words in addressing a Mussulman, even to her husband; invectives are always at her tongue's end; she exhales a bad odour which infects you, and sticks to you even after you have left her.

And not less contemptible is she who talks to no purpose, who is a hypocrite and does no good act; she, who, when her husband asks her to fulfil the conjugal office, refuses to listen to his demand; the woman who does not assist her husband in his affairs; and finally, she who plagues him with unceasing complaints and tears.

A woman of that sort, seeing her husband irritated or in trouble does not share his affliction; on the contrary, she laughs and jests all the more, and does not try to drive away his ill humour by endearments. She is more prodigal with her person to other men than to her husband; it is not for his sake that she adorns herself, and it is not to please him that she tries to look well. Far from that; with him she is very untidy, and does not mind letting him see things and habits about her person which must be repugnant to him. Lastly, she never uses either *Atsmed* nor *Souak*.

No happiness can be hoped for a man with such a wife. God keep us from such a one!

CHAPTER 5

Relating to the Act of Generation

Know, o Vizir (and God protect you!), that if you wish for coition, in joining the woman you should not have your stomach loaded with food and drink, only in that condition will your cohabitation be wholesome and good. If your stomach is full, only harm can come of it to both of you; you will have threatening symptoms of apoplexy and gout, and the least evil that may result from it will be the inability of passing your urine, or weakness of sight.

Let your stomach then be free from excessive food and drink, and you need not apprehend any illness.

Before setting to work with your wife excite her with toying, so that the copulation will finish to your mutual satisfaction.

Thus it will be well to play with her before you introduce your verge and accomplish the cohabitation. You will excite her by kissing her cheeks, sucking her lips and nibbling at her breasts. You will lavish kisses on her navel and thighs, and titillate the lower parts. Bite at her arms, and neglect no part of her body; cling close to her bosom, and show her your love and submission. Interlace your legs with hers, and press her in your arms, for, as the poet has said:

> *Under her neck my right hand has served her for a cushion,*
> *And to draw her to me*
> *I have sent out my left hand,*
> *Which bore her up as a bed.*

When you are close to a woman, and you see her eyes getting dim, and hear her, yearning for coition, heave deep sighs, then let your and her yearning be joined into one, and let your lubricity rise to the highest point; for this will be the moment most favourable to the game of love. The pleasure which the woman then feels will be extreme; as for yourself, you will cherish her all the more, and she will continue her affection for you, for it has been said:

If you see a woman heaving deep sighs, with her lips getting red and her eyes languishing, when her mouth half opens and her movements grow heedless; when she appears to be disposed to go to sleep, vacillating in her steps and prone to yawn, know that this is the moment for coition; and if you there and then make your way into her you will procure for her an unquestionable treat. You yourself will find the mouth of her womb clasping your article, which is undoubtedly the crowning pleasure for both, for this before everything begets affection and love.

The following precepts, coming from a profound connoisseur in love affairs, are well known:

Woman is like a fruit, which will not yield its sweetness until you rub it between your hands. Look at the basil plant; if you do not rub it warm with your fingers it will not emit any scent. Do you not know that the amber, unless it be handled and warmed, keeps hidden within its pores the aroma contained in it. It is the same with woman. If you do not animate her with your toying, intermixed with kissing, nibbling and touching, you will not obtain from her what you are wishing; you will feel no enjoyment when you share her couch, and you will waken in her heart neither inclination nor affection, nor love for you; all her qualities will remain hidden.

It is reported that a man, having asked a woman what means were the most likely to create affection in the female heart, with respect to the pleasures of coition, received the following answer:

O you who question me, those things which develop the taste for coition are the toyings and touches which precede it, and then the close embrace at the moment of ejaculation!

Believe me, the kisses, nibblings, suction of the lips, the close embrace, the visits of the mouth to the nipples of the bosom, and the sipping of the fresh saliva, there are the things to render affection lasting.

In acting thus, the two orgasms take place simultaneously, and enjoyment comes to the man and woman at the same moment. Then the man feels the womb grasping his member, which gives to each of them the most exquisite pleasure.

This it is which gives birth to love, and if matters have not been managed this way the woman has not had her full share of pleasure, and the delights of the womb are wanting. Know that the woman will not feel her desires satisfied, and will not love her rider unless he is able to act up to her womb; but when the womb is made to enter into action she will feel the most violent love for her cavalier, even if he be unsightly in appearance.

Then do all you can to provoke a simultaneous discharge of the two spermal fluids; herein lies the secret of love.

One of the savants who have occupied themselves with this subject has thus related the confidences which one of them made to him:

O you men, one and all, who are soliciting the love of woman and her affection, and who wish that sentiment in her heart to be of an enduring nature, toy with her previous to coition; prepare her for enjoyment, and neglect nothing to attain that end. Explore her with the greater assiduity, and, entirely occupied with her, let nothing else engage your thoughts. Do not let the moment propitious for pleasure pass away; that moment will be when you see her eyes humid, half open. Then go to work, but, remember, not till your kisses and toyings have taken effect.

After you have got the woman into a proper state of excitement, O men! put your member into her, and, if you then observe the proper movements, she will experience a pleasure which will satisfy all her desires.

Lie on her breast, rain kisses on her cheeks, and let not your member quit her vagina. Push for the mouth of her womb. This will crown your labour.

If, by God's favour, you have found this delight, take good care not to with-draw your member, but let it remain there, and imbibe an endless pleasure! Listen to the sighs and heavy breathing of the woman. They witness the violence of the bliss you have given her.

And after the enjoyment is over, and your amorous struggle has come to an end, be careful not to get up at once, but with-draw your member cautiously. Remain close to the woman, and lie down on the right side of the bed that witnessed your enjoyment. You will find this pleasant, and you will not be like a fellow who mounts the woman after the fashion of a mule, without any regard to refinement, and who, after the emission, hastens to get his member out and to rise. Avoid such manners, for they rob the woman of all her lasting delight.

In short, the true lover of coition will not fail to observe all that I have recommended; for, from the observance of my recommendations will result the pleasure of the woman, and these rules comprise everything essential in that respect.

God has made everything for the best!

CHAPTER 6

Concerning Everything that is Favourable to the Act of Coition

Know, o Vizir (God be good to you!), if you would have pleasant coition, which ought to give an equal share of happiness to the two combatants and be satisfactory to both, you must first of all toy with the woman, excite her with kisses, by nibbling and sucking her lips, by caressing her neck and cheeks. Turn her over in the bed, now on her back, now on her stomach, till you see by her eyes that the time for pleasure is near, as I have mentioned in the preceding chapter, and certainly I have not been sparing with my observations thereupon.

Then when you observe the lips of a woman to tremble and get red, and her eyes to becoming languishing, and her sighs to become quicker, know that she is hot for coition; then get between her thighs, so that your member can enter into her vagina. If you follow my advice, you will enjoy a pleasant embrace, which will give you the greatest satisfaction, and leave with you a delicious remembrance.

Someone has said:

If you desire coition, place the woman on the ground, cling closely to her bosom, with her lips close to yours; then clasp her to you, suck her breath, bite her; kiss her breasts, her stomach, her flanks, press her close in your arms, so as to make her faint with pleasure; when you see her so far gone, then push your member into her. If you have done as I said, the enjoyment will come to both of you simultaneously. This it is which makes the pleasure of the woman so sweet. But if you neglect my advice the woman will not be satisfied and you will not have procured her any pleasure.

The coition being finished, do not get up at once, but come down softly on her right side, and if she has conceived, she will bear a male child, if it please God on high!

Sages and Savants (may God grant to all his forgiveness!) have said:

If anyone placing his hand upon the vulva of a woman that is with child pronounces the following words: 'In the name of God! may he grant salutation and mercy to his Prophet (salutation and mercy be with him). Oh! my God! I pray to thee in the name of the Prophet to let a boy issue from this conception,' it will come to pass by the will of God, and in consideration for our lord Mohammed, (the salutation and grace of God be with him), the woman will be delivered of a boy.

Do not drink rain-water directly after copulation, because this beverage weakens the kidneys.

If you want to repeat the coition, perfume yourself with sweet scents, then close with the woman, and you will arrive at a happy result.

Do not let the woman perform the act of coition mounted upon you, for fear that in that position some drops of her seminal fluid might enter the canal of your verge and cause a sharp urethritis.

Do not work hard directly after coition as this might affect your health adversely, but go to rest for some time.

Do not wash your verge directly after having with-drawn it from the vagina of the woman, until the irritation has gone down somewhat; then wash it and its opening carefully. Otherwise, do not wash your member frequently. Do not leave the vulva directly after the emission, as this may cause canker.

Sundry Positions for the Coitus

The ways of doing it to women are numerous and variable. And now is the time to make known to you the different positions which are usual.

God, the magnificent, has said:

'Women are your field. Go upon your field as you like.' According to your wish you can choose the position you like best, provided, of course, that coition takes place in the spot destined for it, that is, in the vulva.

Manner the first—Make the woman lie upon her back, with her thighs raised, then, getting between her legs, introduce your member into her. Pressing your toes to the ground, you can rummage her in a convenient, measured way. This is a good position for a man with a long verge.

Manner the second—If your member is a short one, let the woman lie on her back, lift her legs into the air, so that her right leg be near her right ear, and the left one near her left ear, and in this posture, with her buttocks lifted up, her vulva will project forward. Then put in your member.

44

Manner the third—Let the woman stretch herself upon the ground, and place yourself between her thighs; then putting one of her legs upon your shoulder, and the other under your arm, near the armpit, get into her.

Manner the fourth—Let her lie down, and put her legs on your shoulders; in this position your member will just face her vulva, which must not touch the ground. And then introduce your member.

Manner the fifth—Let her lie down on her side, then lie yourself down by her on your side, and getting between her thighs, put your member into her vagina. But sidelong coition predisposes for rheumatic pains and sciatica.

Manner the sixth—Make her get down on her knees and elbows, as if kneeling in prayer. In this position the vulva is projected backwards; you then attack her from that side, and put your member into her.

Manner the seventh—Place the woman on her side, and squat between her thighs, with one of her legs on your shoulder and the other between your thighs, while she remains lying on her side. Then you enter her vagina, and make her move by drawing her towards your chest by means of your hands, with which you hold her embraced.

Manner the eighth—Let her stretch herself upon the ground, on her back, with her legs crossed; then mount her like a cavalier on horseback, being on your knees, while her legs are placed under her thighs, and put your member into her vagina.

Manner the ninth—Place the woman so that she leans with her front, or, if you prefer it, her back upon a moderate elevation, with her feet set upon the ground. She thus offers her vulva to the introduction of your member.

Manner the tenth—Place the woman near to a low divan, the back of which she can take hold of with her hands; then, getting under her, lift her legs to the height of your navel, and let her clasp you with her legs on each side of your body; in this position plant your verge into her, seizing with your hands the back of the divan. When you begin the action your movements must respond to those of the woman.

Manner the eleventh—Let her lie upon her back on the ground with a cushion under her posterior; then getting between her legs, and letting her place the sole of her right foot against the sole of her left foot, introduce your member.

There are other positions besides the above named in use among the peoples of India. It is well for you to know that the inhabitants of those parts have multiplied the different ways to enjoy women, and they have advanced farther than we in the knowledge and investigation of coitus.

Amongst those manners are the following, called:

1. *El asemeud,* the stopperage.
2. *El modefedâ,* frog fashion.
3. *El mokefâ,* with the toes cramped.
4. *El mokeurmeutt,* with legs in the air.
5. *El setouri,* he-goat fashion.
6. *El loulabi,* the screw of Archimedes.
7. *El kelouci,* the summersault.
8. *Hachou en nekanok,* the tail of the ostrich.
9. *Lebeuss el djoureb,* fitting on of the sock.
10. *Kechef el astine,* reciprocal sight of the posteriors.
11. *Nezâ el kouss,* the rainbow arch.
12. *Nesedj el kheuzz,* alternative piercing.
13. *Dok el arz,* pounding on the spot.
14. *Nik el kohoul,* coition from the back.
15. *El keurchi,* belly to belly.
16. *El kebachi,* ram-fashion.
17. *Dok el outed,* driving the peg home.
18. *Sebek el heub,* love's fusion.
19. *Tred ech chate,* sheep-fashion.
20. *Kalen el miche,* interchange in coition.
21. *Rekeud el aïr,* the race of the member.
22. *El modakheli,* the fitter-in.
23. *El khouariki,* the one who stops in the house.
24. *Nik el haddadi,* the smith's coition.
25. *El moheundi,* the seducer.

FIRST MANNER—*El asemeud* (the stopperage). Place the woman on her back, with a cushion under her buttocks, then get between her legs, resting the points of your feet against the ground; bend her two thighs against her chest as far as you can; place your hands under her arms so as to enfold her or cramp her shoulders. Then introduce your member, and at the moment of ejaculation draw her towards you. This position is painful for the woman, for her thighs being bent upwards and her buttocks raised by the cushion, the walls of her vagina tighten, and the uterus tending forward there is not much room for movement, and scarcely space enough for the intruder; consequently the latter enters with difficulty and strikes against the uterus. This position should therefore not be adopted, unless the man's member is short or soft.

SECOND MANNER—*El modefedâ* (frog fashion). Place the woman on her back, and arrange her thighs so that they touch the heels,

46

which latter are thus coming close to the buttocks; then down you sit in this kind of merry thought, facing the vulva, in which you insert your member; you then place her knees under your arm-pits; and taking firm hold of the upper part of her arms, you draw her towards you at the crisis.

THIRD MANNER—*El mokefâ* (with the toes cramped). Place the woman on her back, and squat on your knees, between her thighs, gripping the ground with your toes; raise her knees as high as your sides, in order that she may cross her legs over your back, and then pass her arms round your neck.

FOURTH MANNER—*El mokeurmeutt* (with legs in the air). The woman lying on her back, you put her thighs together and raise her legs up until the soles of her feet look at the ceiling; then enfolding her within your thighs you insert your member, holding her legs up with your hands.

FIFTH MANNER—*El setouri* (he-goat fashion). The woman being crouched on her side, you let her stretch out the leg on which she is resting, and squat down between her thighs with your calves bent under you; then you lift her uppermost leg so that it rests on your back, and introduce your member. During the action you take hold of her shoulders, or, if you prefer it, by the arms.

SIXTH MANNER—*El loulabi* (the screw of Archimedes). The man being stretched on his back the woman sits on his member, facing him; she then places her hands upon the bed so that she can keep her stomach from touching the man's, and moves up and downwards, and if the man is supple he assists her from below. If in this position she wants to kiss him, she need only stretch her arms along the bed.

SEVENTH MANNER—*El kelouci* (the summersault). The woman must wear a pair of pantaloons, which she lets drop upon her heels; then she stoops, placing her head between her feet, so that her neck is in the opening of her pantaloons. At that moment the man, seizing her legs, turns her upon her back, making her perform a summersault; then with his legs curved under him he brings his member right against her vulva, and, slipping it between her legs, inserts it.

It is alleged that there are women who, while lying on their back, can place their feet behind their head without the help of pantaloons or hands.

EIGHTH MANNER—*Hachou en nekanok* (the tail of the ostrich). The woman lying on her back along the bed, the man kneels in front of her, lifting up her legs until her head and shoulders only are resting on the bed; his member having penetrated into her vagina, he seizes and sets into motion the buttocks of the woman who, on her part, twines her legs around his neck.

NINTH MANNER—*Lebeuss el djoureb* (fitting on of the sock). The woman lies on her back. You sit down between her legs and place your member between the lips of her vulva, which you fit over it with your thumb and first finger; then you move so as to procure for your member, as far as it is in contact with the woman, a lively rubbing, which action you continue until her vulva gets moistened with the liquid emitted from your verge. When she is thus amply prepared for enjoyment by the alternate coming and going of your weapon in her scabbard, put it into her in full length.

TENTH MANNER—*Kechef el astine* (reciprocal sight of the posteriors). The man lying stretched out on his back, the woman sits down upon his member with her back to the man's face, who presses her sides between his thighs and legs, whilst she places her hands upon the bed as a support for her movements, and lowering her head, her eyes are turned towards the buttocks of the man.

ELEVENTH MANNER—*Nezâ el kouss* (the rainbow arch). The woman is lying on her side; the man also on his side, with his face towards her back, pushes in between her legs and introduces his member, with his hands lying on the upper part of her back. As to the woman, she then gets hold of the man's feet, which she lifts up as far as she can, drawing him close to her; thus she forms with the body of the man an arch, of which she is the rise.

TWELFTH MANNER—*Nesedj el kheuzz* (the alternate movement of piercing). The man in sitting attitude places the soles of his feet together, and lowering his thighs, draws his feet nearer to his member; the woman sits down upon his feet, which he takes care to keep firm together. In this position the two thighs of the woman are pressed against the man's flanks, and she puts her arms round his neck. Then the man clasps the woman's ankles, and drawing his feet nearer to his body, brings the woman, who is sitting on them, within range of his member, which then enters her vagina. By moving his feet he sends her back and brings her forward again, without ever with-drawing his member entirely.

The woman makes herself as light as possible, and assists as well as she can in this come-and-go movement; her co-operation is, in fact, indispensable for it. If the man apprehends that his member may come out entirely, he takes her round the waist, and she receives no other impulse than that which is imparted to her by the feet of the man upon which she is sitting.

THIRTEENTH MANNER—*Dok el arz* (pounding on the spot). The

man sits down with his legs stretched out; the woman then places herself astride on his thighs, crossing her legs behind the back of the man, and places her vulva opposite his member, which latter she guides into her vagina; she then places her arms round his neck, and he embraces her sides and waist, and helps her to rise and descend upon his verge. She must assist in his work.

FOURTEENTH MANNER—*Nik el kohoul* (coitus from the back). The woman lies down on her stomach and raises her buttocks by help of a cushion; the man approaches from behind, stretches himself on her back and inserts his tool, while the woman twines her arms round the man's elbows. This is the easiest of all methods.

FIFTEENTH MANNER—*El keurchi* (belly to belly). The man and the woman are standing upright, face to face; she opens her thighs; the man then brings his feet forward between those of the woman, who also advances hers a little. In this position the man must have one of his feet somewhat in advance of the other. Each of the two has the arms round the other's hips; the man introduces his verge, and the two move thus intertwined after a manner called *neza' el dela,* which I shall explain later, if it please God the Almighty. (See FIRST MANNER.)

SIXTEENTH MANNER—*El kebachi* (after the fashion of the ram). The woman is on her knees, with her forearms on the ground; the man approaches from behind, kneels down, and lets his member penetrate into her vagina, which she presses out as much as possible; he will do well in placing his hands on the woman's shoulders.

SEVENTEENTH MANNER—*Dok el outed* (driving the peg home). The woman enlaces with her legs the waist of the man, who is standing, with her arms passed round his neck, steadying herself by leaning against the wall. Whilst she is thus suspended the man insinuates his pin into her vulva.

EIGHTEENTH MANNER—*Sebek el heub* (love's fusion). While the woman is lying on her right side, extend yourself on your left side; your left leg remains extended, and you raise your right one till it is up to her flank, when you lay her upper leg upon your side. Thus her uppermost leg serves the woman as a support for her back. After having introduced your member you move as you please, and she responds to your action as she pleases.

NINETEENTH MANNER—*Tred ech chate* (coitus of the sheep). The woman is on her hands and knees; the man, behind her, lifts her thighs till her vulva is on a level with his member, which he then inserts. In this position she ought to place her head between her arms.

49

TWENTIETH MANNER—*Kaleb el miche* (interchange in coition). The man lies on his back. The woman, gliding in between his legs, places herself upon him with her toe-nails against the ground; she lifts up the man's thighs, turning them against his own body, so that his virile member faces her vulva, into which she guides it; she then places her hands upon the bed by the sides of the man. It is, however, indispensable that the woman's feet rest upon a cushion to enable her to keep her vulva in concordance with his member.

In this position the parts are exchanged, the woman fulfilling that of the man, and vice-versa.

There is a variation to this manner. The man stretches himself out upon his back, while the woman kneels with her legs under her, but between his legs. The remainder conforms exactly to what has been said above.

TWENTY-FIRST MANNER—*Rekeud el aïr* (the race of the member). The man, on his back, supports himself with a cushion under his shoulders, but his posterior must retain contact with the bed. Thus placed, he draws up his thighs until his knees are on a level with his face; then the woman sits down, impaling herself on his member; she must not lie down, but keep seated as if on horseback, the saddle being represented by the knees and the stomach of the man. In that position she can, by the play of her knees, work up and down and down and up. She can also place her knees on the bed, in which case the man accentuates the movement by plying his thighs, whilst she holds with her left hand on to his right shoulder.

TWENTY-SECOND MANNER—*El modakheli* (the fitter-in). The woman is seated on her coccyx, with only the points of her buttocks touching the ground; the man takes the same position, her vulva facing his member. Then the woman puts her right thigh over the left thigh of the man, whilst he on his part puts his right thigh over her left one.

The woman, seizing with her hands her partner's arms, gets his member into her vulva; and each of them leaning alternately a little back, and holding each other by the upper part of the arms, they initiate a swaying movement, moving with little concussions, and keeping their movements in exact rhythm by the assistance of their heels, which are resting on the ground.

TWENTY-THIRD MANNER—*El khouariki* (the one who stops at home). The woman being couched on her back, the man lies down upon her, with cushions held in his hands.

After his member is in, the woman raises her buttocks as high as she can off the bed, the man following her up with his member well inside; then the woman lowers herself again upon the bed, giving some short shocks, and although they do not embrace, the man must stick like glue to her. This movement they continue, but the man must make himself light and must not be ponderous, and the bed must be soft; in default of which the exercise cannot be kept up without break.

TWENTY-FOURTH MANNER—*Nik el haddadi* (the coition of the blacksmith). The woman lies on her back with a cushion under her buttocks, and her knees raised as far as possible towards her chest, so that her vulva stands out as a target; she then guides her partner's member in.

The man executes for some time the usual action of coition, then draws his tool out of the vulva, and glides it for a moment between the thighs of the woman, as the smith with-draws the glowing iron from the furnace in order to plunge it into cold water. This manner is called *sferdgeli*, position of the quince.

TWENTY-FIFTH MANNER—*El moheundi* (the seducer). The woman lying on her back, the man sits between her legs, with his croupe on his feet; then he raises and separates the woman's thighs, placing her legs under his arms, or over his shoulders; he then takes her round the waist, or seizes her shoulders.

The preceding descriptions furnish a large number of procedures, that cannot well be all put to the proof; but with such a variety to choose from, the man who finds one of them difficult to practice, can easily find plenty of others more to his convenience.

I have not made mention of positions which it appeared to me impossible to realize, and if there be anybody who thinks that those which I have described are not exhaustive, he has only to look for new ones.

It cannot be gainsaid that the Indians have surmounted the greatest difficulties in respect to coition. As a grand exploit, originating with them, the following may be cited:

The woman being stretched out on her back, the man sits down on her chest, with his back turned to her face, his knees turned forward and his nails gripping the ground; he then raises her hips, arching her back until he has brought her vulva face to face with his member, which he then inserts, and thus gains his purpose.

This position, as you perceive, is very fatiguing and very difficult to attain. I even believe that the only realization of it consists in words and designs. With regard to the other methods described above, they can only be practised if both man and woman are free from physical defects, and of analogous construction; for instance, one or the other of them must not be humpbacked, or very little, or very tall, or too obese. And I repeat, that both must be in perfect health.

I shall now treat of coition between two persons of different conformation. I shall particularise the positions that will suit them in treating each of them severally.

I shall first discourse of the coition of a lean man and a corpulent woman, and the different postures they may assume for the act, assuming the woman to be lying down, and being turned successively over on her four sides.

If the man wants to work her sideways he takes the thigh of the woman which is uppermost, and raises it as high as possible on his flank, so that it rests over his waist; he employs her undermost arms as a pillow for the support of his head, and he takes care to place a stout cushion beneath his undermost hip, as to elevate his member to the necessary height, which is indispensable on account of the thickness of the woman's thighs.

But if the woman has an enormous abdomen, projecting by reason of its obesity over her thighs and flanks, it will be best to lay her on her back, and to lift up her thighs towards her belly; the man kneels between them, having hold of her waist with his hands, and drawing her towards him; and if he cannot manage her in consequence of the obesity of her belly and thighs, he must with his two arms encircle her buttocks. But it is thus impossible for him to work her conveniently, owing to the want of mobility of her thighs, which are impeded by her belly. He may, however, support them with his hands, but let him take care not to place them over his own thighs, as, owing to their weight, he would not have the power nor the facility to move. As the poet has said:

> If you have to explore her, lift up her buttocks,
> In order to work like the rope thrown to a drowning man.
> You will then seem between her thighs
> Like a rower seated at the end of the boat.

The man can likewise couch the woman on her side, with the undermost leg in front; then he sits down on the thigh of that leg, his member being opposite her vulva, and lets her raise the upper leg, which she must bend at the knee. Then, with his hands seizing her legs and thighs, he introduces his member, with his body lying between her legs, his knees bent, and the points of his feet against the ground, so that he can elevate his posterior, and prevent her thighs from impeding the entrance. In this attitude they can enter into action.

If the woman's belly is enlarged by reason of her being with child, the man lets her lie down on one side; then placing one of her thighs over the other, he raises them both towards the stomach, without their touching the latter; he then lies down behind her on the same side, and can thus fit his member in. In this way he can thrust his tool in entirely, particularly by raising his foot, which is under the woman's leg, to the height of her thigh. The same may be done with a barren woman; but it is particularly to be recommended for the woman who is *enceinte,* as the above position offers the advantage of procuring her the pleasure she desires, without exposing her to any danger.

In the case of the man being obese, with a very pronounced rotundity of stomach, and the woman being thin, the best course to follow is to let the woman take the active part. To this end, the man lies down on his back with this thighs close together, and the woman lowers herself upon his member, astride of him; she rests her hands upon the bed, and he seizes her arms with his hands. If she knows how to move, she can thus, in turn, rise and sink upon his member; if she is not adroit enough for that movement, the man imparts a movement to her buttocks by the play of one of his thighs behind them. But if the man assumes this position, it may sometimes become prejudicial to him, inasmuch as some of the female sperm may penetrate into his urethra, and grave malady may ensue therefrom. It may also happen—and that is just as bad—that the man's sperm cannot pass out, and returns into the urethra.

If the man prefers that the woman should lie on her back, he places himself, with his legs folded under him, between her legs, which she parts only moderately. Thus, his buttocks are between the woman's legs, with his heels touching them. In performing this way he will, however, feel fatigue, owing to the position of his stomach resting upon the woman's, and the inconvenience resulting therefrom; and, besides, he will not be able to get his whole member in the vulva.

It will be similar when both lie on their sides, as mentioned above in the case of pregnant women.

When both man and woman are fat, and wish to unite in coition, they cannot contrive to do it without trouble, particularly when both have prominent stomachs. In these circumstances the best way to go about it is for the woman to be on her knees with her hands on the ground, so that her posterior is elevated; then the man separates her legs, leaving the points of the feet close together and the heels parted asunder; he then attacks her from behind, kneeling and holding up his stomach with his hand, and so introduces his member. Resting his stomach upon her buttocks during the act he holds the thighs or the waist of the woman with his hands. If her posterior is too low for his stomach to rest upon, he must place a cushion under her knees to remedy this.

I know of no other position so favourable as this for the coition of a fat man with a fat woman.

If, in fact, the man gets between the legs of a woman on her back under the above named circumstances, his stomach, encountering the woman's thighs, will not allow him to make free use of his tool. He cannot even see her vulva, or only in part; it may be almost said that it will be impossible for him to accomplish the act.

On the other hand, if the man makes the woman lie upon her side, and then places himself, with his legs bent behind her, press ing his stomach upon the upper part of her posterior, she must draw her legs and thighs up to her stomach, in order to lay bare her vagina and allow the introduction of his member; but if she cannot sufficiently bend her knees, the man can neither see her vulva, nor explore it.

If, however, the stomach of each person is not exaggeratedly large, they can manage very well all positions. Only they must not be too long in coming to the crisis, as they will soon feel fatigued and lose their breath.

In the case of a very big man and a very little woman, the difficulty to be solved is how to contrive that their organs of generation and their mouths can meet at the same time. To gain this end the woman had best lie on her back; the man places himself on his side near her, passes one of his hands under her neck, and with the other raises her thighs till he can put his member against her vulva from behind, the woman remaining still on her back. In this position he holds her up with his hands by the neck and the thighs. He can then enter her body, while the woman on her part puts her arms round his neck, and approaches her lips to his.

If the man wishes the woman to lie on her side, he gets between her legs, and, placing her thighs so that they are in contact with his sides, one above and one under, he glides in between them till his member is facing her vulva from behind; he then presses his thighs against her buttocks, which he seizes with one hand in order to impart movement to them; the other hand he has round her neck. If the man then likes, he can get his thighs over those of the woman, and press her towards him; this will make it easier for him to move.

As regards the copulation of a very small man and a tall woman, the two actors cannot kiss each other while in action unless they

54

take one of the three following positions, and even then they will become fatigued.

First Position—The woman lies on her back, with a thick cushion under her buttocks, and a similar one under her head; she then draws up her thighs as far as possible towards her chest. The man lies down upon her, introduces his member, and takes hold of her shoulders, drawing himself up towards them. The woman winds her arms and legs round his back, whilst he holds on to her shoulders, or, if he can, to her neck.

Second Position—Man and woman lie both on their side, face to face; the woman slips her undermost thigh under the man's flank, drawing it at the same time higher up; she does the like with her other thigh over his; then she arches her stomach out, while his member is penetrating into her. Both should have hold of the other's neck, and the woman, crossing her legs over his back, should draw the man towards her.

Third Position—The man lies on his back, with his legs stretched out; the woman sits on his member, and, stretching herself down over him, draws up her knees to the height of her stomach; then, laying her hands over his shoulders, she draws herself up, and presses her lips to his.

All these postures are more or less fatiguing for both; people can, however, choose any other position they like; but they must be able to kiss each other during the act.

I will now speak to you of those who are little, in consequence of being humpbacked. Of these there are several kinds.

First, there is the man who is crookbacked, but whose spine and neck are straight. For him it is most convenient to unite himself with a little woman, but not otherwise than from behind. Placing himself behind her posterior, he thus introduces his member into her vulva. But if the woman is in a stooping attitude, on her hands and feet, he will do still better. If the woman be afflicted with a hump and the man is straight, the same position is suitable.

If both of them are crookbacked they can take what position they like for coition. They cannot, however, embrace; and if they lie on their side, face to face, there will be left an empty space between them. And if one or the other lies down on the back, a cushion must be placed under the head and the shoulder, to hold them up, and fill the place which is left vacant.

In the case of a man whose malformation affects only his neck, so as to press his chin towards his chest, but who is otherwise straight, he can take any position he likes for doing the business, and give himself up to any embraces and caresses, always excepting kisses on the mouth. If the woman is lying on her back, he will appear in action as if he were butting at her like a ram. If the woman has her neck deformed in similar manner, their coition will resemble the mutual attack of two horned beasts with their heads. The most convenient position for them will be that the woman should stoop down, and he attack her from behind. The man whose hump appears on his back in the shape of only the half of a jar is not so much disfigured as the one of whom the poet has said:

> Lying on his back he is a dish;
> Turn him over, and you have a dish-cover.

In his case coition can take place as with any other man who is small in stature and straight; he cannot, however, easily lie on his back.

If a little woman is lying on her back, with a humpbacked man upon her belly, he will look like the cover over a vase. If, on the contrary, the woman is large-sized, he will have the appearance of a carpenter's plane in action. I have made the following verses on this subject:

> The humpback is vaulted like an arch;
> And seeing him you cry, 'Glory be to God!'
> You ask him how he manages in coitus?
> 'It is the retribution for my sins,' he says.
> The woman under him is like a board of deal;
> The humpback, who explores her, does the planing.

I have also said in verse:

> The humpback's dorsal cord is tied in knots,
> The Angels tire with writing all his sins;
> In trying for a wife of proper shape;
> And for her favours, she repulses him,
> And says, 'Who bears the wrongs we shall commit?'
> And he, 'I bear them well upon my hump!'
> And then she mocks him saying, 'Oh, you plane
> Destined for making shavings! take a deal board!'

If the woman has a hump as well as the man, they may take any of the various positions for coition, always observing that if one of them lies on the back, the hump must be environed with cushion, as with a turban, thus having a nest to lie in, which guards its top, which is very tender. In this way they can embrace closely.

If the man is humped both on back and chest he must renounce the embrace and clinging, but can otherwise take any position he likes for coition. Yet generally speaking, the action must always be troublesome for himself and the woman. I have written on this subject:

> The humpback engaged in the act of coition
> Is like a vase provided with two handles.
> If he is burning for a woman, she will tell him,
> 'Your hump is in the way; you cannot do it;
> Your verge would find a place to rummage in,
> But on your chest the hump, where would it be?'

If both the woman and the man have double humps, the best position they can assume for coitus is the following: 'Whilst the woman is lying on her side, the man introduces his member after the fashion described previously in respect to pregnant women. Thus the two humps do not encounter one another. Both are lying on their sides, and the man attacks from behind. Should the woman be on her back, her hump must be supported by a cushion, whilst the man kneels between her legs, she holding up her posterior. Thus placed, their two humps are not near each other, and all inconvenience is avoided.

The same is the case if the woman stoops down with her head, with her croup in the air, after the manner of *El kouri*, which position will suit both of them, if they have the chest malformed, but not the back. One of them then performs the action of come-and-go.

But the most curious and amusing description which I have ever met in this respect, is contained in these verses:

> Their two extremities are close together,
> And nature made a laughing stock of them;
> Foreshortened he appears as if cut off;
> He looks like someone bending to escape a blow,
> Or like a man who has received a blow
> And shrivels down so as to miss a second.

If a man's spine is curved about the hips and his back is straight, so that he looks as though he was in prayer, half prostrated, coition for him is very difficult; owing to the reciprocal positions of his thighs and his stomach, he cannot possibly insert his member entirely, as it lies so far back between his thighs. The best for him to do is to stand up. The woman stoops down before him with her hands to the ground, and her posterior in the air; he can thus introduce his member as a pivot for the woman to move upon, for, be it observed, he cannot well move himself. It is the manner *El kouri,* with the difference, that it is the woman who moves.

57

A man may be attacked by the illness called *ikaad,* or *zomana* (paralysis), which compels him to be constantly seated. If this malady only affects his knees and legs, his thighs and spinal column remaining sound, he can use all the sundry positions for coition, except those where he would have to stand up. In the case of his buttocks being affected, even if he is otherwise perfectly well, it is the woman who will have to make all the movements.

Know that the most enjoyable coitus does not always exist in the manners described here; I only give them, so as to render this work as complete as possible. Sometimes most enjoyable coition takes place between lovers, who, not quite perfect in their proportions, find their own means for their mutual gratification.

It is said that there are women of great experience who, lying with a man, elevate one of their feet vertically in the air, and upon that foot a lamp is set full of oil, and with the wick burning. While the man is ramming them, they keep the lamp steady and burning, and the oil is not spilled. Their coition is in no way impeded by this exhibition, but it must require great previous practice on the part of both.

Assuredly the Indian writers have in their works described a great many ways of making love, but the majority of them do not yield enjoyment, and give more pain than pleasure. That which is to be looked for in coition, the crowning point of it, is the enjoyment, the embrace, the kisses. This is the distinction between the coitus of men and that of animals. No one is indifferent to the enjoyment which proceeds from the difference between the sexes, and man finds his highest felicity in it.

If the desire of love in man is roused to its highest pitch, all the pleasures of coition become easy for him, and he satisfies his yearning in any way.

It is well for the lover of coition to put all these manners to the proof, so as to ascertain which is the position that gives the greatest pleasure to both combatants. Then he will know which to choose for the tryst, and in satisfying his desires retain the woman's affection.

Many people have essayed all the positions I have described but none has been as much approved of as the *Dok el arz.*

A story is told on this subject of a man who had a wife of incomparable beauty, graceful and accomplished. He used to explore her in the ordinary manner, never having recourse to any other. The woman experienced none of the pleasure which ought to accompany the act, and was consequently generally very moody after the coition was over.

The man complained about this to an old dame, who told him, 'Try different ways in uniting yourself to her, until you find the one which best satisfies her. Then work her in this fashion only, and her affection for you will know no limit.'

He then tried upon his wife various manners of coition, and when he came to the one called *Dok el arz* he saw her overcome by violent transports of love, and at the crisis of pleasure he felt her womb grasp his verge energetically; and she said to him, biting his lips, 'This is the veritable manner of making love!'

These demonstrations proved to the lover, in fact, that his mistress felt in that position the most lively pleasure, and he always thenceforward worked with her in that way. Thus he attained his end, and caused the woman to love him to folly.

Therefore try different manners; for every woman likes one in preference to all other for her pleasure. The majority of them have, however, a predilection for the *Dok el arz*, as, in the application of the same, belly is pressed to belly, mouth glued to mouth, and the action of the womb is rarely absent.

I have now only to mention the various movements practised during coitus, and shall describe some of them.

First Movement—Neza el dela (the bucket in the well). The man and woman join in close embrace after the introduction. Then he gives a push, and with-draws a little; the woman follows him with a push, and also retires. So they continue their alternate movement, keeping proper time. Placing foot against foot, and hand against hand, they keep up the motion of a bucket in a well.

Second Movement—El netahi (the mutual shock). After the introduction, they each draw back, but without dislodging the member completely. Then they both push tightly together, and thus go on keeping time.

Third Movement—El motadani (the approach). The man moves as usual, and then stops. Then the woman, with the member in her receptacle, begins to move like the man, and then stops. And they continue this way until the ejaculation comes.

Fourth Movement—Khiate el heub (Love's tailor). The man, with his member being only partially inserted in the vulva, keeps up a sort of quick friction with the part that is in, and then suddenly plunges his whole member in up to its root. This is the movement of the needle in the hands of the tailor, of which the man and woman must take cognisance.

Such a movement only suits those men and women who can at

will retard the crisis. With those who are otherwise constituted it would act too quickly.

Fifth Movement—Souak el feurdj (the toothpick in the vulva). The man introduces his member between the walls of the vulva, and then drives it up and down, and right and left. Only a man with a very vigorous member can execute this movement.

Sixth Movement—Tâchik el heub (the boxing up of love). The man introduces his member entirely into the vagina, so closely that his hairs are completely mixed up with the woman's. In that position he must now move forcibly, without with-drawing his tool in the least.

This is the best of all the movements, and is particularly well adapted to the position *Dok el arz*. Women prefer it to any other kind, as it procures them the extreme pleasure of seizing the member with their womb; and appeases their lust most completely.

Those women called *tribades* always use this movement in their mutual caresses. And it provokes prompt ejaculation both with man and woman.

Without kissing, no kind of position or movement procures the fullest pleasure; and those positions in which the kiss is not practicable are not entirely satisfactory, considering that the kiss is one of the most powerful stimulants to the work of love.

I have said in verse:

> *The languishing eye*
> *Puts in connection soul with soul,*
> *And the tender kiss*
> *Takes the message from member to vulva.*

The kiss is assumed to be an integral part of coition. The best kiss is the one impressed on humid lips combined with the suction of the lips and tongue, which latter particularly provokes the flow of sweet and fresh saliva. It is for the man to bring this about by slightly and softly nibbling his partner's tongue, when her saliva will flow sweet and exquisite, more pleasant than refined honey, and which will not mix with the saliva of her mouth. This manoeuvre will give the man a trembling sensation, which will run all through his body, and is more intoxicating than wine drunk to excess.

A poet has said:

> *In kissing her, I have drunk from her mouth*
> *Like a camel that drinks from the redir;*
> *Her embrace and the freshness of her mouth*
> *Give me a languor that goes to my marrow.*

60

The kiss should be sonorous; it originates with the tongue touching the palate, lubricated by saliva. It is produced by the movement of the tongue in the mouth and by the displacement of the saliva, provoked by the suction.

The kiss given to the superficial outer part of the lips, and making a noise comparable to the one by which you call your cat, gives no pleasure. It is well enough thus applied to children and hands.

The kiss I have described above is the one for coitus and is full of voluptuousness.

A vulgar proverb says:

> A humid kiss
> Is better than a hurried coitus.

I have composed on this subject the following lines:

> You kiss my hand—my mouth should be the place!
> O woman, thou who art my idol!
> It was a fond kiss you gave me, but it is lost,
> The hand cannot appreciate the nature of a kiss.

The three words, *Kobla, letsem,* and *bouss* are used indifferently to indicate the kiss on the hand or on the mouth. The word *ferame* means specially the kiss on the mouth.

An Arab poet has said:

> The heart of love can find no remedy
> In witching sorcery nor amulets,
> Nor in the fond embrace without a kiss,
> Nor in a kiss without coitus.

And the author of the work, 'The Jewels of the Bride and the Rejoicing of Souls,' has added to the above, as complement and commentary, the two following verses:

> Nor in converse, however unrestrained,
> But in the placing of legs on legs (coition).

Remember that all caresses and all sorts of kisses, as described, are of no account without the introduction of the member. Therefore abstain from them, if you do not want action; they only fan a fire to no purpose. The passion which is excited resembles in fact a fire which is being lighted; and just as water only can extinguish the latter, so only the emission of the sperm can calm the lust and appease the heat.

The woman is not more advantaged than the man by caresses without coition.

It is said that Dahama ben Mesedjel appeared before the Governor of the province of Yamama, with her father and her husband, El Adjadje, alleging that the latter was impotent, and did not cohabit with her nor come near her.

Her father, who assisted her in her case, was reproached for mixing himself up with her plaint by the people of Yamama, who said to him, 'Are you not ashamed to help your daughter in bringing a claim for coition?'

To which he answered, 'It is my wish that she should have children; if she loses them it will be by God's will; if she brings them up they will be useful to her.'

Dahama formulated her claim thus in coming before the Governor: 'There stands my husband, and until now he has never touched me.' The Governor interposed, saying, 'No doubt this is because you have been unwilling?' 'On the contrary,' she replied, 'it is for him that I open my thighs and lie down on my back.' Then cried the husband, 'O Emir, she tells untruth; in order to possess her I have to fight with her.' The Emir pronounced the following judgment: 'I give you,' he said, 'a year's time to prove her allegation to be false.' He decided thus out of regard for the man. El Adjadje then went away reciting those verses:

Dahama and her father Mesedjel thought
The Emir would decide upon my impotence.
Is not the stallion sometimes lazy-minded?
And yet he is so large and vigorous.

Returned to his house he began to kiss and caress his wife; but his efforts went no farther, he remained incapable of giving proofs of his virility. Dahama said to him, 'Keep your caresses and embraces; they do not satisfy love. What I desire is a solid and stiff member, the sperm of which will flow into my matrix.' And she recited to him the following verses:

Before God! it is in vain to try with kisses
To entertain me, and with your embracings!
To still my torments I must feel a member,
Ejaculating sperm into my uterus.

El Adjadje, in despair, conducted her forthwith back to her family, and, to hide his shame, repudiated her that very night.

A poet said on that occasion:

62

What are caresses to an ardent woman,
Or costly vestments and fine jewellery,
If the man's organs do not meet her own,
And she is yearning for the virile verge?

Know then that the majority of women do not find full satisfaction in kisses and embraces without coition. For them satisfaction resides only in the member, and they like the man who rummages them, even if he is ugly and misshapen.

A story also goes on this subject that Moussa ben Mesâb betook himself one day to a woman in the town who had a female slave, an excellent singer, whom he wanted to buy from her. This woman was resplendently beautiful, and independent of her charming appearance, she had a large fortune. He saw at the same time in the house a young man of bad shape and ungainly appearance, who went to and fro giving orders.

Moussa having asked who the man was, she told him, 'This is my husband, and for him I would give my life!' 'This is a hard slavery,' he said, 'to which you are reduced, and I am sorry for you. We belong to God, and shall return to him! but what a misfortune it is that such incomparable beauty and such delightful forms as I see in you should be for such a man!'

She made answer, 'O son of my mother, if he could do to you from behind what he does for me in front, you would sell your lately acquired fortune as well as your patrimony. He would appear to you beautiful, and his plain looks would be changed into beauty.'

'May God preserve him to you!' said Moussa.

It is also said that the poet Farazdak met one day a woman on whom he cast a glance burning with love, and who for that reason thus addressed him: 'What makes you look at me in this fashion? Had I a thousand vulvas, there would be nothing to hope for you!' 'And why?' said the poet. 'Because your appearance is not prepossessing,' she said, 'and what you keep hidden will be no better.' He replied, 'If you would put me to the proof, you would find that my interior qualities are of a nature to make you forget my outer appearance.' He then uncovered himself, and let her see a member the size of the arm of a young girl. At that sight she felt herself burning hot with amorous desire. He saw this, and asked her to let him caress her. Then she uncovered herself and showed him her mount of Venus, vaulted like a cupola. He then did the business for her, and recited these verses:

I have plied in her my member, big as a virgin's arm;
A member with a round head, and prompt to attack;

Measuring in length a span and a half,
And, oh! I felt as though I had put it in a brazier.

He who seeks the pleasure a woman can give must satisfy her amorous desire for hot caresses, as described. He will see her swooning with lust, her vulva will get moist, her womb will stretch forward, and the two sperms will come together.

CHAPTER 7

Of Matters which are Injurious in the Act of Generation

Know, O Vizir (to whom God be good!), that the ills caused by coition are numerous. I will mention to you some of them, which to know is essential, in order to be able to avoid them.

Let me tell you in the first place that coition, if performed standing, affects the knee-joints and brings about nervous shiverings; and if performed sideways will predispose your system for gout and sciatica, which resides chiefly in the hip joint.

Do not mount upon a woman fasting or immediately before making a meal, or else you will have pains in your back, you will lose your vigour, and your eyesight will get weaker.

If you do it with the woman bestriding you, your dorsal cord will suffer and your heart will be affected; and if in that position the smallest drop of the usual secretions of the vagina enters your urethral canal, a painful stricture may supervene.

Do not leave your member in the vulva after ejaculation, as this might cause gravel, or softening of the vertebral column, or the rupture of blood vessels, or lastly, inflammation of the lungs.

Too much exercise after coition is also detrimental.

Avoid washing your member after the copulation, as this may cause canker.

As to coition with old women, it acts like a fatal poison, and it has been said, 'Do not rummage old women, were they as rich as Karoun.' And it has further been said, 'Beware of mounting old women; and if they cover you with favours.' And again, 'The coitus of old women is a venomous meal.'

Know that the man who works a woman younger than he is himself acquires new vigour; if she is of the same age as he is he will derive no advantage from it; and, finally, if it is a woman older than himself she will take all his strength out of him for herself. The following verses treat on this subject:

Be on your guard and shun coition with old women;
In her bosom she bears the poison of the arakime.

A proverb says also, 'Do not serve an old woman, even if she offered to feed you with semolina and almond bread.'

The excessive practice of coition injures the health on account of the expenditure of too much sperm. For as butter made of cream represents the quintessence of the milk, and if you take the cream off, the milk loses its qualities, even so does the sperm form the quintessence of nutrition, and its loss is debilitating. On the other hand, the condition of the body, and consequently the quality of the sperm depends directly upon the food you take. If, therefore, a man will passionately give himself up to the enjoyment of coition, without undergoing too great fatigue, he must live upon strengthening food, exciting comfits, aromatic plants, meat, honey, eggs, and other similar viands. He who follows such a régime is protected against the following accidents, to which excessive coition may lead.

Firstly, the loss of generative power.

Secondly, the deterioration of his sight; for although he may not become blind, he will at least have to suffer from eye diseases if he does not follow my advice.

Thirdly, the loss of his physical strength; he may become like the man who wants to fly but cannot, who pursuing somebody cannot catch him, or who carrying a burden, or working, soon gets tired and prostrated.

He who does not want to feel the necessity for coition uses camphor. Half of a *mitskal* of this substance, macerated in water, makes the man who drinks of it insensible to the pleasures of copulation. Many women use this remedy when in fits of jealousy against rivals, or when they need repose after great excesses. Then they try to procure camphor that has been left after a burial, and shrink from no expense of money to get such from the old women who have the charge of the corpses. They also make use of the flower of henna, which is called faria; they macerate the same in water, until it turns yellow, and thus supply themselves with a beverage which has almost the same effect as camphor.

I have treated of these remedies in the present chapter, although this is not their proper place; but I thought that this information, as here given, may be of use to many persons.

There are certain things which will become injurious if constantly indulged in and which in the end affect the health. Such are: too much sleep, long voyages in unfavourable season, which latter, particularly in cold countries, may weaken the body and cause disease of the spine. The same effects may arise from the habitual handling of those bodies which engender cold and humidity, like plaster, etc.

66

For people who have difficulty in passing water coitus is hurtful. The habit of consuming acid food is debilitating.

To keep one's member in the vulva of a woman after ejaculation has taken place, be it for a long or a short time, enfeebles that organ and makes it less fit for coition.

If you are lying with a woman, do her business several times if you feel inclined, but take care not to overdo it, for it is a true word that 'He who plays the game of love for his own sake, and to satisfy his desires, feels the most intense and durable pleasure; but he who does it to satisfy the lust of another person will languish, lose all his desire, and finish by becoming impotent for coition.'

The sense of these words is, that a man when he feels disposed for it can give himself up to the exercise of coitus with more or less ardour according to his desires, and at the time which best suits him, without any fear of future impotence, if his enjoyment is provoked and regulated only by his feeling the want of lying with a woman.

But he who makes love for the sake of somebody else, that is to say only to satisfy the passion of his mistress, and tries all he can to attain that impossibility, that man will act against his own interest and imperil his health to please another person.

As injurious may be considered coition in the bath or immediately after leaving the bath; after having been bled or purged or such like. Coitus after a heavy bout of drinking is likewise to be avoided. To indulge coitus with a woman during her courses is as detrimental to the man as to the woman herself, as at that time her blood is vitiated and her womb cold, and if the least drop of blood should get in the man's urinary canal numerous maladies may supervene. As to the woman, she feels no pleasure during her courses, and at such time holds coitus in aversion.

As regards copulation in the bath, some say that there is no pleasure to be derived from it, if, as is believed, the degree of enjoyment is dependent upon the warmth of the vulva; for in the bath the vulva cannot be otherwise than cold, and consequently unfit for giving pleasure. And it is besides not to be forgotten that the water penetrating into the sexual parts of man or woman may lead to grave consequences.

Coitus after a full meal may occasion rupture of the intestines. It is also to be avoided after undergoing much fatigue, or at a time of very hot or very cold weather.

Amongst the accidents which may attend the act of coition in hot countries may be mentioned sudden blindness without any previous symptoms.

The repetition of the coitus without washing the parts ought to be shunned, as it may enfeeble the virile power.

The man must also abstain from copulation with his wife if he is in a state of legal impurity, for if she should become pregnant by such coition the child could not be sound.

After ejaculation do not remain close to the woman, as the disposition for recommencing will suffer by doing so.

Care is to be taken not to carry heavy loads on one's back or to over-exert the mind, if one does not want the coitus to be impeded. It is also not good constantly to wear vestments made of silk, as they impair all the energy for copulation. Silken cloths worn by women also affect injuriously the capacity for erection of the virile member.

Fasting, if prolonged, calms sexual desire; but in the beginning it excites the same.

Abstain from greasy liquids, as in the course of time they diminish the strength necessary for coition.

The effect of snuff, whether plain or scented, is similar.

It is bad to wash the sexual parts with cold water directly after copulation; in general, washing with cold water calms down the desire, while warm water strengthens it.

Conversation with a young woman excites in a man the erection and passion commensurate with the youthfulness of the woman.

An Arab addressed the following recommendation to his daughter at the time when he conducted her to her husband: 'Perfume yourself with water!' meaning that she should frequently wash her body with water in preference to perfumes; the latter, moreover, not being suitable for everyone.

It is also reported that a woman having said to her husband, 'You are then a nobody, as you never perfume yourself!' he made answer, 'Oh, you sloven! it is for the woman to emit a sweet odour.'

The abuse of coition is followed by loss of the taste for its pleasures; and to remedy this loss the sufferer must anoint his member with a mixture of the blood of a he-goat with honey. This will procure for him a marvellous effect in making love.

It is said that reading the Koran also predisposes for copulation.

Remember that a prudent man will beware of abusing the enjoyment of coition. The sperm is the water of life; if you use it economically you will always be ready for love's pleasures; it is the light of your eye; do not be lavish with it at all times and whenever you have a fancy for enjoyment, for if you are not sparing with it you will expose yourself to many ills. Wise medical men say, 'A robust constitution is indispensable for copulation, and he

68

who is endowed with it may give himself up to the pleasure without danger; but it is otherwise with the weakly man; he runs into danger by indulging freely with women.'

The sage, Es Sakli, has thus determined the limits to be observed by man as to the indulgence of the pleasures of coition: Man, be he phlegmatic or sanguine, should not make love more than twice or thrice a month; bilious or hypochondriac men only once or twice a month. It is nevertheless a well established fact that nowadays men of any of these four temperaments are insatiable as to coition, and give themselves up to it day and night, taking no heed how they expose themselves to numerous ills, both internal and external.

Women are more favoured than men in indulging their passion for coition. It is in fact their specialty; and for them it is all pleasure; while men run many risks in abandoning themselves without reserve to the pleasures of love.

Having thus treated of the dangers which may occur from the coitus, I have considered it useful to bring to your knowledge the following verses, which contain hygienic advice in their respect. These versus have been composed by the order of Haroun er Rachid by the most celebrated physicians of his time, whom he had asked to inform him of the remedies for successfully combating the ills caused by coition.

> *Eat slowly, if your food shall do you good,*
> *And take good care, that it be well digested.*
> *Beware of things which want hard mastication;*
> *They are bad nourishment, so keep from them.*
> *Drink not directly after finishing your meal,*
> *Or else you go half way to meet an illness.*
> *Keep not within you what is of excess,*
> *And if you were in most susceptible circles,*
> *Attend to this well before seeking your bed,*
> *For rest this is the first necessity.*
> *From medicines and drugs keep well away,*
> *And do not use them unless very ill.*
> *Use all precautions proper, for they keep*
> *Your body sound, and are the best support.*
> *Don't be too eager for round-breasted women;*
> *Excess of pleasure soon will make you feeble,*
> *And in coition you may find a sickness;*
> *And then you find too late that in coition*
> *Our spring of life runs into woman's vulva.*
> *And before all beware of aged women,*

For their embraces will to you be poison.
Each second day a bath should wash you clean;
Remember these precepts and follow them.

Those were the rules given by the sages to the master of benevolence and goodness, to the generous of the generous.

All sages and physicians agree in saying that the ills which afflict man originate with the abuse of coition. The man therefore who wishes to preserve his health, and particularly his sight, and who wants to lead a pleasant life, will indulge with moderation in love's pleasures, aware that the greatest evils may spring therefrom.

CHAPTER 8

The Sundry Names given to the Sexual Parts of Man

Know, O Vizir (to whom God be good!), that man's member bears different names, as:

El de keur, the virile member.
El kamera, the penis.
El aïr, the member for generation.
El hamama, the pigeon.
El teunnana, the tinkler.
El heurmak, the indomitable.
El ahlil, the liberator.
El zeub, the verge.
El hammache, the exciter.
El nâasse, the sleeper.
El zodamme, the crowbar.
El khiade, the tailor.
Mochefi el relil, the extinguisher of passion.
El khorrate, the turnabout.
El deukkak, the striker.
El âouame, the swimmer.
El dekhal, the housebreaker.
El âouar, the one-eyed.
El fortass, the bald.
Abou aïne, the one with an eye.
El atsar, the pusher.
El dommar, the strong-headed.
Abou rokba, the one with a neck.
Abou quetaïa, the hairy one.
El besiss, the impudent one.
El mostahi, the shame-faced one.
El bekkaï, the weeping one.
El hezzaz, the rummager.
El lezzaz, the unionist.

Abou lâaba, the expectorant.
El fattache, the searcher.
El hakkak, the rubber.
El mourekhi, the flabby one.
El motelá, the ransacker.
El mokcheuf, the discoverer.

Dekeur is a word which signifies the male of all creatures, and is also used in the sense of 'mention' and 'memory.' When a man has met with an accident to his member, when it has been amputated, or has become weak, and he can, in consequence, no longer fulfil his conjugal duties, they say of him: 'the member of such an one is dead;' which means: the remembrance of him will be lost, and his generation is cut off by the root. When he dies they will say, 'His member has been cut off.'

The *dekeur* plays also an important part in dreams. The man who dreams that his member has been cut off is certain not to live long after that dream.

To dream of the coriander (*keusbeur*) signifies that the vulva (*keuss*) is in proper condition.

On this subject there is a story that the Sultan Haroun er Rachid having with him several persons with whom he was familiar, left them to go to one of his wives, whom he wanted to enjoy. He found her suffering from her courses, and returned to his companions, resigned to his disappointment.

Now it so happened that a moment afterwards the woman found herself free from her discharge. She made forthwith her ablutions, and sent to the Sultan a plate of coriander.

He took it and examined it, but did not understand the meaning. At last he handed it to one of his poets, who, having looked at it attentively, recited to him the following verses:

> *She has sent you coriander* (keusbeur);
> *I have concentrated all my thoughts upon it,*
> *In order to find out its meaning;*
> *And I have seized it. O my master, what she wants to say,*
> *Is 'My vulva is restored to health'* (keussi beuri).

A long beard points to good fortune and prosperity.

Others pretend that the intelligence of each man is in an inverse proportion to the length of his beard. A story goes that a man who had a long beard saw one day a book with the following sentence inscribed: 'He whose chin is garnished with a large beard is as foolish as his beard is long.' Afraid of being taken for a fool, he thought of getting rid of what there was too much of, and grasped

72

a handful of his beard close to the chin, and set the remainder on fire by the light of the lamp. The flame ran rapidly up the beard and reached his hand, which he had to withdraw precipitately on account of the heat. Thus his beard was burnt off entirely. Then he wrote on the back of the book, 'These words are entirely true. I, who am writing this, have proved their truth.'

On the same subject it is related that Haroun er Rachid, being in a kiosk, saw a man with a long beard. He asked him, 'What is your name?' 'Abou Arouba,' replied the man.

Haroun then gave him the following case to solve. A man buys a he-goat, who, in voiding his excrements, hits the buyer's eye with part of it and injures the same. 'Who has to pay for damages?' 'The seller,' promptly says Abou Arouba. 'And why?' asked the Kalif. 'Because he has sold the animal without warning the buyer that it has a catapult in its anus,' answered the man.

I now return to the object of this chapter, viz: the different names of the sexual parts of man.

The name of *el aïr* is derived from *el kir* (the smith's bellows). In fact if you turn the k, *kef,* so that it faces the opposite way, you will find the word to read *el aïr*. The member is so called on account of its alternate swelling and subsiding again. If swollen up it stands erect, and if not it sinks down flaccid.

It is called *el hamama* (the pigeon), because after having been swelled out it resembles at the moment when it returns to repose a pigeon sitting on her eggs.

El teunnana (the tinkler)—So called because every time it enters or comes out of the vulva in coition it makes a noise.

El heurmak (the indomitable)—It has received this name because when in a state of erection it begins to move its head, searching for the entrance to the vulva till it has found it, and it then walks in quite insolently, without asking leave.

El ahlil (the liberator)—Thus called because in penetrating into the vulva of a woman thrice repudiated it gives her the liberty to return to her first husband.

El zeub (the verge)—From the word *deub,* which means creeping. This name was given to the member because when it gets between a woman's thighs and feels a plump vulva it begins to creep upon the thighs and the Mount of Venus, then approaches the entrance of the vulva, and keeps creeping in until it is in possession and is comfortably lodged, and having it all its own way penetrates into the middle of the vulva, there to ejaculate.

El hammache (the exciter)—It has received this name because it irritates the vulva by its frequent entries and exits.

El ndasse (the sleeper)—From its deceitful appearance. When it gets into erection, it lengthens out and stiffens itself to such an extent that one might think it would never get soft again. But when it has left the vulva, after having satisfied its passion, it goes to sleep.

There are members that fall asleep while inside the vulva, but the majority of them come out still firm; but at that moment they get drowsy, and little by little they go to sleep.

El zoddame (the crowbar)—It is called so because when it meets the vulva and the same will not let it pass in directly, it forces the entrance with its head, breaking and tearing everything, like a wild beast in the rutting season.

El khiate (the tailor)—It takes this name from the circumstance that it does not enter the vulva until it has manoeuvred about the entrance, like a needle in the hand of a tailor, creeping and rubbing against it until it is sufficiently roused, after which it enters.

Mochefi el relil (the extinguisher of passion)—This name is given to a member which is large, strong, and slow to ejaculate; such a member satisfies most completely the amorous wishes of a woman; for, after having wrought her up to the highest pitch, it allays her excitement better than any other. And, in the same way, it calms the ardour of the man. When it wants to get into the vulva, and arriving at the portal, finds it closed, it laments, begs and promises: 'Oh! my love! let me come in, I will not stay long.' And when it has been admitted, it breaks its word, and makes a long stay, and does not take its leave till it has satisfied its ardour by the ejaculation of the sperm, coming and going, tilting high and low, and rummaging right and left. The vulva protests, 'How about your word, you deceiver?' she says; 'you said you would only stop in for a moment.' And the member answers, 'Oh, certainly! I shall not retire till I have encountered your womb; but after having found it, I will engage to with-draw at once.' At these words, the vulva takes pity on him, and advances her matrix, which clasps and kisses its head, as if saluting it. The member then retires with its passion cooled down.

El khorrate (the turnabout)—This name was given to it because on arriving at the vulva it pretends to come on important business, knocks at the door, turns about everywhere, without shame or bashfulness, investigating every corner to the right and left, forward and backward, and then all at once darts right to the bottom of the vagina for the ejaculation.

El deukkak (the striker)—Thus called because on arriving at the entrance of the vulva it gives a slight knock. If the vulva opens the door, it enters; if there is no response, it begins to knock again, and does not cease until it is admitted. The parasite who wants to get

74

into the house of a rich man to be present at a feast does the same: he knocks at the door; and if it is opened, he walks in; but if there is no response to his knock, he repeats it again and again until the door is opened. And similarly the *deukkak* with the door of the vulva.

By 'knocking at the door' is meant the friction of the member against the entrance of the vulva until the latter becomes moist. The appearance of this moisture is the phenomenon alluded to by the expression 'opening the door.'

El douame (the swimmer)—Because when it enters the vulva it does not remain in one favourite place, but, on the contrary, turns to the right, to the left, goes forward, draws back, and then moves like swimming in the middle amongst its own sperm and the fluid furnished by the vulva, as if in fear of drowning and trying to save itself.

El dekhal (the housebreaker)—Merits that name because on coming to the door of the vulva this one asks, 'What do you want?' 'I want to come in!' 'Impossible! I cannot take you in on account of your size.' Then the member insists that the other one should only receive its head, promising not to come in entirely; it then approaches, rubs its head twice or thrice between the vulva's lips, till they get humid and thus lubricated, then introduces first its head, and after, with one push, plunges in up to the testicles.

El adouar (the one-eyed)—Because it has but one eye, which eye is not like other eyes, and does not see clearly.

El fortass (the bald one)—Because there is no hair on its head, which makes it look bald.

Abou aïne (he with one eye)—It has received this name because its one eye presents the peculiarity of being without pupil and eyelashes.

El atsar (the stumbler)—It is called so because if it wants to penetrate in the vulva, as it does not see the door, it beats about above and below, and thus continues to stumble as over stones in the road, until the lips of the vulva get humid, when it manages to get inside. The vulva then says, 'What has happened to you that made you stumble about so?' The member answers, 'O my love, it was a stone lying in the road.'

El dommar (the odd-headed)—Because its head is different from all other heads.

Abou rokba (the one with a neck)—That is the being with a short neck, a well developed throat, and thick at the end, a bald head, and who, moreover, has coarse and bristly hair from the navel to the pubis.

75

Abou guetaïa (the hairy one; who has a forest of hair)—This name is given to it when the hair is abundant about it.

El besiss (the impudent)—It has received this name because from the moment that it gets stiff and long it does not care for anybody, lifts impudently the clothing of its master by raising its head fiercely, and makes him ashamed while itself feels no shame. It acts in the same unabashed way with women, turning up their clothes and laying bare their thighs. Its master may blush at this conduct, but as to itself its stiffness and determination to plunge into a vulva only increase.

El mostahi (the shame-faced)—This sort of member which is met with sometimes, is capable of feeling ashamed and timid when facing a vulva which it does not know, and it is only after a little time that it gets bolder and stiffens. Sometimes it is even so much troubled that it remains incompetent for the coitus, which happens in particular when a stranger is present, in which case it becomes quite incapable of moving.

El bekkai (the weeper)—So called on account of the many tears it sheds; as soon as it gets in erection, it weeps; when it sees a pretty face, it weeps; handling a woman, it weeps. It goes even so far as to weep tears sacred to memory.

El hezzaz (the rummager)—It is named thus because as soon as it penetrates into the vulva it begins to rummage about vigorously, until it has appeased its passion.

El lezzaz (the unionist)—Received that name because as soon as it is in the vulva it pushes and works till fur meets fur, and even makes efforts to force the testicles into it.

Abou lâaba (the expectorant)—Has received this name because when coming near a vulva, or when it sees one, or even when merely thinking of it, or when its master touches a woman or plays with her or kisses her, its saliva begins to move and it has tears in its eye; this saliva is particularly abundant when it has been for some time out of work, and it will even wet then his master's dress. This member is very common, and there are but few people who are not furnished with it.

The liquid it sheds is cited by lawyers under the name of *medi.* Its production is the result of toyings and of lascivious thoughts. With some people it is so abundant as to fill the vulva, so that they may erroneously believe that it comes from the woman.

El fattache (the searcher)—From its habit, when in the vulva, of turning in every direction as if in search of something; and that something is the matrix. It will know no rest until it has found it.

El hakkak (the rubber)—It has got this name because it will not enter the vagina until it has rubbed its head against the entrance

76

and the lower part of the belly. It is frequently mistaken for the next one.

El mourekhi (the flabby one)—The one who can never get in because it is too soft, and which is therefore content to rub its head against the entrance to the vulva until it ejaculates. It gives no pleasure to woman, but only inflames her passion without being able to satisfy it, and makes her cross and irritable.

El motelâ (the ransacker)—So named because it penetrates into unusual places, makes itself well acquainted with the state of vulvas, and can distinguish their qualities and faults.

El mokcheuf (the discoverer)—Has been thus denominated because in getting up and raising its head, it raises the vestments which hide it, and uncovers its master's nudities, and because it is also not afraid to lay bare the vulvas which it does not yet know, and to lift up the clothes which cover them without shame. It is not accessible to any sense of bashfulness, cares for nothing and respects nothing. Nothing which concerns the coitus is strange to it; it has a profound knowledge of the state of humidity, freshness, dryness, tightness or warmth of vulvas, which it explores assiduously. There are, in fact, certain vulvas of an exquisite exterior, plump and fine outside, while their inside leaves much to wish for, and they give no pleasure, owing to their being not warm, but very humid, and having other similar faults. It is for this reason that the *mokcheuf* tries to find out about things concerning the coitus, and has received this name.

These are the principal names that have been given to the virile member according to its qualities. Those who think that the number of these names is not exhaustive can look for more; but I think I have given a nomenclature long enough to satisfy my readers.

CHAPTER 9

Sundry Names given to the Sexual Organs of Women

El feurdj, the slit.
El keuss, the vulva.
El kelmoune, the voluptuous.
El ass, the primitive.
El zerzour, the starling.
El cheukk, the chink.
Abou tertour, the one with a crest.
Abou khochime, the one with a little nose.
El gueunfond, the hedgehog.
El sakouti, the silent one.
El deukkak, the crusher.
El tseguil, the importunate.
El taleb, the yearning one.
El hacene, the beautiful.
El neuffakh, the one that swells.
Abou djebaha, the one with a projection.
Elouasâ, the vast one.
El dride, the large one.
Abou beldoum, the glutton.
El mokaour, the bottomless.
Abou cheufrine, the two lipped.
Abou âungra, the humpbacked.
El rorbal, the sieve.
El hezzaz, the restless.
El lezzaz, the unionist.
El moudd, the accommodating.
El moudïne, the assistant.
El meusboul, the long one.
El molki, the duellist.
El harrab, the fugitive.
El sabeur, the resigned.
El moseuffah, the barred one.

El mezour, the deep one.
El addad, the biter.
El menssass, the sucker.
El zeunbur, the wasp.
El harr, the hot one.
El ladid, the delicious one.

As regards the vulva called *el feurdj*, the slit, it has this name because it opens and shuts again when hotly yearning for coitus, like the one of a mare in heat at the approach of the stallion.

The person who dreams of having seen the vulva, *feurdj*, of a woman will know that 'if he is in trouble God will free him of it; if he is in a perplexity he will soon get out of it; and lastly if he is in poverty he will soon become wealthy.'

It is considered more lucky to dream of the vulva as open. But if the one seen belongs to a young virgin it indicates that the door of consolation will remain closed, and the thing which is desired is not obtainable. It is a proved fact that the man who sees in his dream the vulva of a virgin will not be lucky in his affairs. But if the vulva is open so that he can look well into it, or even if it is hidden but he is free to enter it, he will bring the most difficult tasks to a successful end.

He who has seen in his dream a man busy upon a young girl, and when the same is getting off her managed to see at that moment her vulva, will bring his business to a happy end. If it is himself who did the girl's business, and he has seen her vulva, he will succeed by his own exertions to realize the most difficult problems, and be successful in every respect. Generally speaking, to see the vulva in dreams is a good sign; so it is of good augury to dream of coition, and he who sees himself in the act, and finishing with the ejaculation, will meet success in all his affairs. But it is not the same with the man who merely begins coition and does not finish it. He, on the contrary, will be unlucky in every enterprise.

It is supposed that the man who dreams of being busy with a woman will afterwards obtain from her what he wants.

The man who dreams of cohabiting with women with whom to have sexual intercourse is forbidden by religion, as for instance his mother, sister, etc., (*maharine*), must consider this as a presage that he will go to sacred places (*moharreme*); and, perhaps, even journey to the holy house of God, and look there upon the grave of the Prophet.

The window (*taga*) and the shoe (*medassa*) reminds you of women. The vulva resembles in fact, when invaded by the verge, a window with a man putting his head in to look about, or a shoe that is being put on. Consequently, he who sees himself in dreaming in the act of getting in at a window, or putting on a shoe, has the certainty of getting possession of a young woman or a virgin, if the window is newly built, or the shoe new and in good condition; but that the woman will be old according to the state of the window or shoe.

El keuss (the vulva)—This word serves as the name of a young woman's vulva in particular. Such a vulva is very plump and round in every direction, with long lips, grand slit, the edges well divided and symmetrical and rounded; it is soft, seductive, perfect throughout. It is the most pleasant and no doubt the best of all the different sorts. May God grant us the possession of such a vulva! Amen. It is warm, tight, and dry; so much so that one might expect to see fire burst out from it. Its form is graceful, its odour pleasant; the whiteness of its outside sets off its carmine-red middle. There is no imperfection about it.

El relmoune (the voluptuous)—The name given to the vulva of a young virgin.

El ass (the primitive)—This is a name applicable to every kind of vulva.

El zerzour (the starling)—The vulva of a very young girl, or, as others pretend, of a brunette.

El cheukk (the chink)—The vulva of a bony, lean woman. It is like a chink in a wall, with not a vestige of flesh. May God keep us from it!

Abou tertour (the crested one)—It is the name given to a vulva furnished with a red comb, like that of a cock, which rises at the moment of enjoyment.

Abou khochime (the snubnose)—Is a vulva with thin lips and a small tongue.

El gueunfond (the hedgehog)—The vulva of the old, decrepit woman, dried up with age and with bristly hair.

El sakouti (the silent one)—This name has been given to the vulva that is noiseless. The member may enter it a hundred times a day but it will not say a word, and will be content to look on without a murmur.

El deukkak (the crusher)—So called from its crushing movements upon the member. It generally begins to push the member, directly it enters, to the right and to the left, and to grip it with the matrix, and would, if it could, absorb also the two testicles.

El tseguil (the importunate)—This is the vulva which is never tired of taking in the member. This latter might pass a hundred nights with it, and walk in a hundred times every night, still that vulva would not be sated—nay, it would want still more, and

80

would not allow the member to come out again at all, if it was possible. With such a vulva the parts are exchanged; the vulva is the pursuer, the member the pursued. Luckily it is a rarity, and only found in a small number of women, who are wild with passion, all on fire, and in flame.

El taleb (the yearning one)—This vagina is met with in a few women only. With some it is natural; with others it becomes what it is by long abstinence. It is burning for a member, and, having got one in its embrace, it refuses to part with it until its fire is completely extinguished.

El hacene (the beautiful)—This is the vulva which is white, plump, in form vaulted like a dome, firm, and without any deformity. You cannot take your eyes off it, and to look at it changes a feeble erection into a strong one.

El neuffakh (the swelling one)—So called because a torpid member coming near it, and rubbing its head against it a few times, at once swells and stands upright. To the woman who has such a one it procures excessive pleasure, for, at the moment of the crisis, it opens and shuts convulsively, like the vulva of a mare.

Abou djebaha (one with a projection)—Some women have this sort of vulva, which is very large, with a pubis prominent like a projecting, fleshy forehead.

El ouasa (the vast one)—A vulva surrounded by a very large pubis. Women of that build are said to be of large vagina, because, although on the approach of the member it appears firm and impenetrable to such a degree that not even a *meroud* seems likely to be passed in, as soon as it feels the friction of the glans against its centre it opens wide at once.

El aride (the large one)—This is the vulva which is as wide as it is long; that is to say, fully developed all round, from side to side, and from the pubis to the perineum. It is the most beautiful to look upon. As the poet has said:

It has the splendid whiteness of a forehead,
In its dimensions it is like the moon,
The fire that radiates from it is like the sun's,
And seems to burn the member which approaches;
Unless first moisted with saliva the member cannot enter,
The odour it emits is full of charms.

It is also said that this name applies to the vagina of women who are plump and fat. When such a one crosses her thighs one over the other the vulva stands out like the head of a calf. If she lays it bare it resembles a *sad* for corn placed between her thighs; and, if she walks, it is apparent under her clothes by its wavy movement at each step. May God, in his goodness and generosity, let us enjoy such a vagina! It is of all the most pleasing, the most celebrated, the most wished for.

Abou beláoum (the glutton)—The vulva with a vast capacity for swallowing. If such a vulva has not been able to get coitus for some time it fairly engulfs the member that then comes near it, without leaving any trace of it outside, like as a man who is famished flings himself upon viands that are offered to him, and would swallow them without mastication.

El mokáour (the bottomless)—This is the vagina of indefinite length, having, in consequence, the matrix lying very far back. It requires a member of the largest dimensions; any other could not succeed in rousing its amorous sensibilities.

Abou cheufrine (the two lipped)—This name is given to the amply developed vagina of an excessively stout woman. Also to the vagina the lips of which having become flaccid, owing to weakness, are long and pendulous.

Abou áungra (the humpbacked)—This vulva has the mount of Venus prominent and hard, standing out like the hump on the back of the camel, and reaching down between the thighs like the head of a calf. May God let us enjoy such a vulva! Amen!

El rorbal (the sieve)—This vulva on receiving a member seems to sift it all over, below, right and left, fore and aft, until the moment of pleasure arrives.

El hezzaz (the restless)—When this vagina has received the member it begins to move violently and without interruption until the member touches the matrix, and then knows no repose till it has hastened on the enjoyment and finished its work.

El lezzaz (the unionist)—The vagina which, having taken in the member, clings to it and pushes itself forward upon it so closely that, if the thing were possible, it would enfold the two testicles.

El moudd (the accommodating)—This name is applied to the vagina of a woman who has felt for a long time an ardent wish for coition. In rapture with the member it sees, it is glad to second its movements of come and go; it offers its matrix to the member by pressing it forward within reach, which is, after all, the best gift it can offer. Whatever place inside of it the member wants to explore, this vulva will make him welcome to, gracefully according to its wish; there is no corner it will not help the member to reach.

El mouáine (the assistant)—This vulva is thus named because it assists the member to go in and out, to go up and down, in short, in all its movements, in such a way that if it desires to do a thing, to enter or to retire, to move about, etc., the vulva hastens to give

82

it all facilities, and answers to its appeal. By this aid the ejaculation is facilitated, and the enjoyment heightened.

El meusboul (the long one)—This name applies only to some vulvas; everyone knows that vulvas are far from being all of the same conformation and aspect. This vulva extends from the pubis to the anus. It lengthens out when the woman is lying down or standing, and contracts when she is sitting, differing in this respect from the vulva of a round shape. It looks like a splendid cucumber lying between the thighs. With some women it shows projecting under light clothing, or when they are bending back.

El molki (the duellist)—This is the vulva which, on the introduction of a member, executes the movement of coming and going, pushes itself upon it for fear of its retiring before the pleasure arrives. There is no enjoyment for it but the shock given to its matrix by the member, and it is for this that it projects its matrix to grip and suck the member's gland when the ejaculation takes place. Certain vulvas, wild with desire and lust, be it natural or a consequence of long abstention, throw themselves upon the approaching member, opening the mouth like a famished infant to whom the mother offers the breast. In the same way this vulva advances and retires upon the member to bring it face to face with the matrix, as if in fear that, unaided, it could not find the same.

The vulva and the member resemble thus two skilful duellists, each time that one of them rushes upon its antagonist, the latter opposes its shield to parry the blow and repulse the assault. The member represents the sword, and the matrix the shield. The one who first ejaculates the sperm is vanquished; while the one who is slowest is the victor; and, assuredly, it is a fine fight! I should like thus to fight without stopping to the day of my death.

As the poet says:

> *I have let them see the effect of a subtle shadow,*
> *Spinning like an ever busy spider.*
> *They said to me, 'How long will you go on?'*
> *I answered them, 'I will work till I am dead.'*

El harrab (the fugitive)—The vagina which, being very tight and short, is hurt by the penetration of a very large and stiff member; it tries to escape to the right and left. It is thus, people say, with the vagina of most virgins, which, not yet having made the acquaintance of the member and fearful of its approach, tries to get out of its way, when it glides in between the thighs and wants to be admitted.

El sabeur (the resigned)—This is the vulva which, having admitted the member, submits patiently to all its whims and movements. It is also said that this vulva is strong enough to suffer resignedly the most violent and prolonged coitions. If it were assaulted a hundred times it would not be vexed or annoyed; and instead of venting reproaches, it would give thanks to God. It will show the same patience if it has to do with several members who visit it successively.

This kind of vagina is found in women of a glowing temperament. If they only knew how to do it, they would not allow the man to dismount, nor his member to retire for a single moment.

El moseuffah (the barred one)—This kind of vagina is not often met with. The defect which distinguishes it is sometimes natural, sometimes it is the result of an unskilfully executed operation of circumcision upon the woman. It can happen that the operator makes a false move with his instrument and injures the two lips, or even only one of them. In healing there forms a thick scar, which bars the passage, and in order to make the vagina accessible to the member, a surgical operation and the use of the bistouri will have to be resorted to.

El merour (the deep one)—The vagina which always has the mouth open, and the bottom of which is beyond sight. The longest members only can reach it.

El âddad (the biter)—The vulva which, when the member has got into it and is burning with passion, opens and shuts again upon the same fiercely. It is chiefly when the ejaculation is coming that the man feels the head of his member bitten by the mouth of the matrix. And certainly there is an attractive power in the same when it clings, yearning for sperm, to the gland, and draws it in as far as it can. If God in his power has decreed that the woman shall become pregnant the sperm gets concentrated in the matrix, where it is gradually vivified; but if, on the contrary, God does not permit the conception, the matrix expels the seed, which then runs over the vagina.

El meusass (the sucker)—This is a vagina which in its amorous heat in consequence of voluptuous toyings, or of long abstinence, begins to suck the member which has entered it so forcibly as to deprive it of all its sperm, dealing with it as a child drawing on the breast of the mother.

The poets have described it in the following verses:

She—the woman—shows in turning up her robe
An object—the vulva—developed full and round,
In semblance like a cup turned upside down.
In placing thereupon your hand, you seem to feel
A well formed bosom, springy, firm, and full.

In boring in your lance it gets well bitten,
And drawn in by a suction, as the breast is by a child.
And after having finished, if you wish to re-commence,
You'll find it flaming hot as any furnace.

Another poet (may God grant all his wishes in Paradise!) has composed on the same theme the following lines:

Like to a man extended on his chest, she—the vulva—fills the hand
Which has to be well stretched to cover it.
The place it occupies is standing forth
Like an unopened bud of the blossom of a palm tree.
Assuredly the smoothness of its skin
Is like the beardless cheek of adolescence;
Its conduit is but narrow,
The entrance to it is not easy,
And he who essays to get in
Feels as though he was butting against a coat of mail.
And at the introduction it emits a sound
Like to the tearing of a woven stuff.
The member having filled its cavity,
Receives the lively welcome of a bite,
Such as the nipple of the nurse receives
When placed between the nursling's lips for suction.
Its lips are burning,
Like a fire that is lighted,
And how sweet it is, this fire!
How delicious for me.

El zeunbour (the wasp)—This kind of vulva is known by the strength and roughness of its fur. When the member approaches and tries to enter it gets sung by the hairs as if by a wasp.

El harr (the hot one)—This is one of the most praiseworthy vulvas. Warmth is in fact very much esteemed in a vulva, and it may be said that the intensity of the enjoyment afforded by it is in proportion to the heat it develops.

Poets have praised it in the following verses:

The vulva possesses an intrinsic heat;
Shut in a solid heart (interior) and pent up breast (matrix).
Its fire communicates itself to him that enters it;
It equals in intensity the fire of love.
She is as tight as a well-fitting shoe,
Smaller than the circle of the apple of the eye.

El ladid (the delicious)—It has the reputation of procuring an unexampled pleasure, comparable only to the one felt by the beasts and birds of prey, and for which they fight sanguinary combats. And if such effects are produced upon animals, what must they be for man? And so it is that all wars spring from the search of the voluptuous pleasure which the vagina procures, and which is the highest fortune of the world; it is a part of the delights of paradise awarded to us by God as a foretaste of what is waiting for us, namely, delights a thousand times superior, and above which only the sight of the Benevolent (God) is to be placed.

More names might certainly be found applicable to the sexual organs of woman, but the number of those mentioned above appears to me ample. The principal object of this work is to collect together all the remarkable and attractive matters concerning coitus, so that he who is in trouble may find consolation in it, and the man to whom erection offers difficulties may be able to look into it for a remedy against his weakness. Wise physicians have written that people whose members have lost their strength, and are afflicted with impotence, should assiduously read books treating of coition, and study carefully the different kinds of lovemaking, in order to recover their former vigour. A certain means of provoking erection is to look at animals in the act of coition. As it is not always everywhere possible to see animals whilst in the act of copulation, books on the subject of generation are indispensable. In every country, large or small, both the rich and poor have a taste for this sort of book, which may be compared to the stone of philosophy transforming common metals into gold.

It is related (and God penetrates the most obscure matters, and is most wise!) that once upon a time, there lived a buffoon, who was the amusement of women, old people and children. His name was Djoâidi. Many women granted him their favours freely, and he was much liked and well received by all. At that time, indeed, any man that was a buffoon enjoyed the greatest consideration, for which reason the poet has said:

Oh, Time! Of all the dwellers here below
You only elevate buffoons or fools,
Or him whose mother was a prostitute,
Or him whose anus as an inkstand serves,
Or him who from his youth has been a pander;
Who has no other work but to bring the two sexes together.

Djoâidi related the following story:

I was in love with a woman who was all grace and perfection, beautiful of shape, and gifted with all imaginable charms. Her cheeks were like roses, her forehead lily white, her lips like coral; she had teeth like pearls, and breasts like pomegranates. Her mouth opened round like a ring; her tongue seemed to be incrusted with precious gems; her eyes, black and finely slit, had the languor of slumber, and her voice the sweetness of sugar. With her form pleasantly filled out, her flesh was mellow like fresh butter, and pure as the diamond.

As to her vulva, it was white, prominent, round as an arch; the centre of it was red, and breathed fire, without a trace of humidity; for, sweet to the touch, it was quite dry. When she walked it showed in relief like a dome or an inverted cup. In reclining it was visible between her thighs, looking like a kid couched on a hillock.

This woman was my neighbour. All the others played and laughed with me, jested with me, and met my suggestions with great pleasure. I revelled in their kisses, their close embraces and nibblings, and in sucking their lips, breasts, and necks. I had coition with all of them, except my neighbour, and it was exactly her I wanted to possess in preference to all the rest; but instead of being kind to me, she avoided me rather. When I contrived to take her aside to trifle with her and try to rouse her gaiety, and spoke to her of my desires, she recited to me the following verses, the sense of which was a mystery to me:

> *Among the mountain tops I saw a tent placed firmly,*
> *Apparent to all eyes high up in mid-air.*
> *But, oh! the pole that held it up was gone.*
> *And like a vase without a handle it remained,*
> *With all its cords undone, its centre sinking in,*
> *Forming a hollow like that of a kettle.*

Every time I told her of my passion she answered me with these verses, which to me were void of meaning, and to which I could make no reply, which, however, only excited my love all the more. I therefore inquired of all those I knew the meaning, but not one of them could solve the riddle for me, so as to satisfy my heat and appease my passion.

At last I heard of a savant named Abou Nouass. I betook myself to him, apprised him of the discourses I had with the woman, and recited the verses.

Abou Nouass said to me, 'This woman loves you to the

exclusion of every other man. She is very corpulent and plump.' I answered, 'It is exactly as you say. You have given her likeness as if she were before you, excepting in respect of her love for me, for she has never given me any proof of it.'

Then he added, 'I have reason to believe that your member is of small dimensions, and such a member cannot give her pleasure nor quench her fire; for what she wants is a lover with a member like that of an ass. Tell me the truth about this!' When I had reassured him on that point, affirming that my member, which began to rise at the expression of his doubtings, was full-sized, he told me that in that case all difficulties would disappear, and explained the sense of the verses as follows:

The *tent,* firmly planted, represents the vulva of grand dimension and placed well forward, the *mountains,* between which it rises, are the thighs. The *stake* which supported its centre and has been torn up, means that she has no husband, comparing the stake or pole that supports the tent to the virile member holding up the lips of the vulva. *She is like a vase without a handle;* this means if the pail is without a handle to hang it up by it is good for nothing, the pail representing the vulva, and the handle the verge. *The cords are undone and its centre is sinking in;* that is to say, as the tent without a supporting pole caves in at the centre, so can the woman who has no husband not enjoy complete happiness. From the words, *It forms a hollow like that of a kettle,* you may judge how lascivious God has made that woman in her comparisons; she likens her vulva to a kettle, which serves to prepare the *tserid.* Listen; if the *tserid* is placed in the kettle, to turn out well it must be stirred by means of a *medeleuk* long and solid. Only in that way can it be properly prepared. It cannot be done with a small spoon; the cook would burn her hands, owing to the shortness of the handle, and the dish would not be well prepared. This is the symbol of this woman's nature, O Djoâidi. If your member has not the dimensions of a respectable *medeleuk,* serviceable for the good preparation of the *tserid,* it will not give her satisfaction, and, moreover, if you do not hold her close to your chest, enlacing her with your hands and feet, it is useless to solicit her favours; finally if you let her consume herself by her own fire, like the bottom of the kettle, which gets burnt if the *medeleuk* is not stirred upon it, you will not gratify her desire by the result.

You see now what prevented her from acceding to your wishes; she was afraid that you would not be able to quench her flame after having fanned it.

88

'Return to her,' said the sage, 'and take her these verses, and your affair will come to a happy issue, please God!'

I understand your words, and all shall see how I obey them.
O you! beloved and cherished by whoever
Can revel in your charms and glory in them!
O apple of my eye! You thought I was embarrassed
About the answer which I had to give you.
Yes, certainly! It was the love I bore you
Made me look foolish in the eyes of all you know.
They thought I was possessed of a demon;
called me a Merry Andrew and buffoon.
For God! What of buffoonery I've got,
*   Should it be that*
No other member is like mine? Here! see it, measure it!
What woman tastes it falls in love with me,
In violent love. It is a well known fact
That you from far may see it like a column.
If it erects itself it lifts my robe and shames me.
Now take it kindly, put it in your tent,
Which is between the well known mountains placed.
It will be quite at home there, you will find it
Not softening while inside, but sticking like a nail;
Take it to form a handle to your vase.
Come and examine it, and notice well
How vigorous it is and long in its erection!
If you but want a proper medeleuk,
A medeleuk *to use between your thighs,*
Take this to stir the centre of your kettle.
It will do good to you, O mistress mine!
Your kettle be it plated will be satisfied!

Having learnt these verses by heart, I took my leave of Abou Nouass and returned to Fadehat el Djemal. She was, as usual, alone. I gave a knock at her door; she came out at once, beautiful as the rising sun, and coming up to me, she said, 'Oh! enemy of God, what business has brought you to me at this time?'

I answered her, 'O my mistress! a business of great importance.'

'Explain yourself, and I will see whether I can help you.'

'I shall not speak to you about it until the door is locked,' I answered.

'Your boldness today is very great,' she said.

And I, 'True, O my mistress! boldness is one of my qualities.'

She then addressed me thus, 'O enemy of yourself! O you most miserable of your race! If I were to lock the door, and you have nothing wherewith to satisfy my desires, what should I do with you? face of a Jew!'

'You will let me share your couch, and grant me your favours.'

She began to laugh; and after we had entered the house, she told a slave to lock the house door. As usual, I asked her to respond to my proposals; she then recited to me again the above mentioned verses. When she had finished I began to recite to her those which Abou Nouass had taught me.

As I proceeded I saw her more and more moved, I observed her giving way, to yawn, to stretch herself, to sigh. I knew now I should arrive at the desired result. When I had finished my member was in such a state of erection that it became like a pillar, still lengthening. When Fadehat el Djemal saw it in that condition she precipitated herself upon it, took it into her hands, and drew it towards her thighs. I then said, 'O apple of my eyes! this may not be done here, let us go into your chamber.'

She replied, 'Leave me alone, O son of a debauched woman! Before God! I am losing my senses in seeing your member getting longer and longer, and lifting your robe. Oh, what a member! I never saw a finer one! Let it penetrate into this delicious, plump vulva, which maddens all who heard it described; for the sake of which so many died of love; and of which your superiors and masters themselves could not get possession.'

I repeated, 'I shall not do it anywhere else than in your chamber.'

She answered, 'If you do not enter this minute this tender vulva I shall die.'

As I still insisted upon repairing to her room, she cried, 'No, it is quite impossible; I cannot wait so long!'

I saw in fact her lips tremble, her eyes filling with tears. A general tremor ran over her, she changed colour, and laid herself down upon her back, baring her thighs, the whiteness of which made her flesh appear like crystal tinged with carmine.

Then I examined her vulva—a white cupola with a purple centre, soft and charming. It opened like that of a mare on the approach of a stallion.

At that moment she seized my member and kissed it, saying, 'By the religion of my father! it must penetrate into my vulva!' and drawing nearer to me she pulled it towards her vagina.

I now hesitated no longer to assist her with my member, and placed it against the entrance to her vulva. As soon as the head of my member touched the lips, the whole body of Fadehat el Djemal trembled with excitement. Sighing and sobbing, she held me pressed to her bosom.

90

Again I profited by this moment to admire the beauties of her vulva. It was magnificent, its purple centre setting off its whiteness all the more. It was round, and without any imperfection; projecting like a splendidly curved dome over her belly. In one word, it was a masterpiece of creation as fine as could be seen. The blessing of God, the best creator, upon it.

And the woman who possessed this wonder had in her time no superior.

Seeing her then in such transports, trembling like a bird, the throat of which is being cut, I pushed my dart into her. But thinking she might not be able to take in the whole of my member, I had entered cautiously, but she moved her buttocks furiously, saying to me, 'This is not enough for my contentment.' Making a strong push, I lodged my member completely in her, which made her utter a painful cry, but the moment after she moved with greater fury than before. She cried, 'Do not miss the corners, neither high nor low, but above all things do not neglect the centre! The centre!' she repeated. 'If you feel it coming, let it go into my matrix so as to extinguish my fire.' Then we moved alternately in and out, which was delicious. Our legs were interlaced, our muscles unbent, and so we went on with kisses and claspings until the crisis came upon us simultaneously. We then rested and took breath after this mutual conflict.

I wanted to with-draw my member, but she would not consent to this and begged of me not to take it out. I acceded to her wish, but a moment later she took it out herself, dried it, and replaced it in her vulva. We renewed our game, kissing, pressing, and moving in rhythm. After a short time, we rose and entered her chamber, without having this time accomplished the enjoyment. She gave me now a piece of an aromatic root, which she recommended me to keep in my mouth, assuring me that as long as I had it there my member would remain on the alert. Then she asked me to lie down, which I did. She mounted upon me, and taking my member into her hands, she made it enter entirely into her vagina. I was astonished at the vigour of her vulva and at the heat emitted from it. The opening of her matrix in particular excited my admiration. I never had any experience like it; it closely clasped my member and pinched the gland.

With the exception of Fadehat el Djemal no woman had until then taken in my member to its full length. She was able to do so, I believe, owing to her being very plump and corpulent, and her vulva being large and deep.

Fadehat el Djemal, astride upon me, began to rise and descend; she kept crying out, wept, went slower, then accelerated her movements again, ceased to move altogether; when part of my member became visible she looked at it, then took it out altogether to examine it closely, then plunged it in again until it had disappeared completely. So she continued until the enjoyment overcame her again. At last, having dismounted from me, she now laid herself down, and asked me to get on to her. I did so, and she introduced my member entirely into her vulva.

We thus continued our caresses, changing our positions in turns, until night came on. I thought it proper to show a wish to go now, but she would not agree to this, and I had to give her my word that I would remain. I said to myself, 'This woman will not let me go at any price, but when daylight comes God will advise me.' I remained with her, and all night long we kept caressing each other, and took but scanty rest.

I counted that during that day and night, I accomplished twenty-seven times the act of coition, and I became afraid that I should nevermore be able to leave the house of that woman.

Having at last made good my escape, I went to visit Abou Nouass again, and informed him of all that had happened. He was surprised and stupefied, and his first words were, 'O Djoâidi, you can have neither authority nor power over such a woman, and she would make you do penance for all the pleasure you have had with other women!'

However, Fadehat el Djemal proposed to me to become her legitimate husband, in order to put a stop to the vexatious rumours that were circulating about her conduct. I, on the other hand, was only on the look out for adultery. Asking the advice of Abou Nouass about it, he told me, 'If you marry Fadehat el Djemal you will ruin your health, and God will with-draw his protection from you, and the worst of all will be that she will cuckold you, for she is insatiable with respect to the coitus, and would cover you with shame.' And I answered him, 'Such is the nature of women; they are insatiable as far as their vulvas are concerned, and so long as their lust is satisfied they do not care whether it be with a buffoon, a negro, a valet, or even with a man that is despised and reprobated by society.'

On this occasion Abou Nouass depicted the character of women in the following verses:

> Women are demons, and were born as such;
> No one can trust them, as is known to all;
> If they love a man, it is only out of caprice;
> And he to whom they are most cruel loves them most.
> Beings full of treachery and trickery, I aver

The man that loves you truly is a lost man;
He who believes me not can prove my word
By letting woman's love get hold of him for years!
If in your own generous mood you have given them
Your all and everything for years and years,
They will say afterwards, 'I swear by God! my eyes
Have never seen a thing he gave me!'
After you have impoverished yourself for their sake,
Their cry from day to day will be for ever 'Give!
Give man, Get up and buy and borrow.'
If they cannot profit by you they'll turn against you;
They will tell lies about you and calumniate you.
They do not recoil to use a slave in the master's absence,
If once their passions are aroused, and they play tricks;
Assuredly, if once their vulva is in rut,
They only think of getting in some member in erection.
Preserve us, God! from woman's trickery;
And of old women in particular. So be it.

CHAPTER 10

Concerning the Organs of Generation of Animals

Know, O Vizir (God's blessing be with you!), that the sexual organs of the various male animals are not analogous with the different natures of the virile members which I have mentioned.

The verges of animals are classed according to the species to which they belong, and these species are four in number.

1. The verges of animals with hoofs, as the horse, mule, ass, which verges are of large size.

El rermoul, the colossus.
El kass, the serpent rolled up.
El fellag, the splitter.
El zellate, the club.
El heurmak, the indomitable.
El meunefoukh, the swollen.
Abou dommar, the one with a head.
Abou beurnita, the one with a hat.
El keurkite, the pointed staff.
El keuntra, the bridge.
El rezama, the mallet.
Abou sella, the fighter.

2. The verges of animals which have the kind of feet called *akhefaf*, as, for instance, the camel.

El mâloum, the well-known.
El tonil, the long one.
El cherita, the riband.
El mostakime, the firm one.
El heurkal, the swinging one.
El mokheubbi, the hidden one.
El châaf, the tuft.
Tsequil el ifaha, the slow-coach.

3. The verges of animals with split hoofs, like the ox, the sheep, etc.

El aceub, the nerve.
El heurbadj, the rod.
El sonte, the whip.
Requig er ras, the small head.
El tonil, the long one.
　　For the ram.
El aïçoub, the nervous.

And lastly, the members of animals with claws, as the lion, fox, dog, and other animals of this species.

El kedib, the verge.
El kibouss, the great gland.
El metemerole, the one that will lengthen.

It is believed that of all the animals of God's creation the lion is the most expert in respect to coition. If he meets the lioness he examines her before copulation. He will know if she has already been covered by a male. When she comes to him he smells at her, and if she has allowed herself to be crossed by a boar he knows it immediately by the odour that animal has left upon her. He then smells her urine, and if the examination proves unfavourable, he gets into a rage, and begins to lash with his tail right and left. Woe to the animal that comes at that time near him; it is certain to be torn to pieces. He then returns to the lioness, who, seeing that he knows all, trembles with terror. He smells again at her, utters a roar which makes the mountains shake, and, falling upon her, lacerates her back with his claws. He even will go so far as to kill her, and then befoul her body with his urine.

It is said that the lion is the most jealous and most intelligent of all animals. It is also averred that he is generous, and spares him who gets round him by fair words.

A man who on meeting a lion uncovers his sexual parts causes him to take flight.

Whoever pronounces before a lion the name of Daniel (Hail be to him!), also sends him flying, because the prophet (Hail be to him!) has enjoined this upon the lion in respect to the invocation of his name. Therefore, when this name is pronounced, the lion departs without doing any harm. Several cases which prove this fact are cited.

CHAPTER 11

On the Deceits and Treacheries of Women

Know, O Vizir (to whom God be good!) that the stratagems of women are numerous and ingenious. Their tricks will deceive Satan himself, for God, the Highest has said (Koran, chapter xii., verse 28), that the deceptive faculties of women are great, and he has likewise said (Koran, chapter vi., verse 38), that the stratagems of Satan are weak. Comparing the word of God as to the ruses of Satan and woman, contained in those two verses, it is easy to see how great these latter ones are.

Story of a Deceived Husband being Convicted Himself of Infidelity

It is related that a man fell in love with a woman of great beauty, and possessing all perfections imaginable. He had made many advances to her, which were repulsed; then he had endeavoured to seduce her by rich presents, which were likewise declined. He lamented, complained, and was prodigal with his money in order to conquer her, but to no purpose, and he grew lean as a spectre.

This lasted for some time, when he made the acquaintance of an old woman, whom he took into his confidence, complaining bitterly about it. She said to him, 'I shall help you, please God.'

Forthwith she made her way to the house of the woman, but the neighbours told her that she could not get in, because the house was guarded by a ferocious bitch, which did not allow anyone to come in or to depart, and in her malignity always flew at the faces of people.

Hearing this, the old woman said to herself, 'I shall succeed, please God.' She then went home, filled a basket with bits of meat, returned to the woman's house, and went in.

The bitch rose to spring at her; but she produced the basket with its contents. As soon as the brute saw the viands, it showed its satisfaction by the movements of its tail and nostrils. The old woman spoke to it as follows, 'Eat, O my sister. Your absence has been painful to me; I did not know what had become of you, and I have been looking for you a long time. Appease your hunger!'

While the animal was eating, and she stroked its back, the mistress of the house came to see who was there, and was not a little surprised to see the bitch, which would never suffer anybody to come near her, so friendly with a strange person. She said, 'O old woman, how is it that you know our dog?' The old woman gave no reply, but continued to caress the animal, and utter lamentations.

Then said the mistress of the house to her, 'My heart aches to see you thus. Tell me the cause of your sorrow.'

'This bitch,' said the woman, 'was formerly a woman, and my best friend. One fine day she was invited with me to a wedding. On our way we were accosted by a man, who at her sight was seized with the most violent love; but she would not listen to him. Then he offered brilliant presents, which she also declined. This man, meeting her some days later, said to her, "Surrender yourself to my passion, or else I shall conjure God to change you into a bitch." She answered, "Conjure as much as you like." The man then called the maledictions of heaven upon that woman, and she was changed into a bitch, as you see here.'

At these words the mistress of the house began to cry and lament, saying, 'O, my mother! I am afraid that I shall meet the same fate as this bitch.' 'Why, what have you done?' said the old woman. The other answered, 'There is a man who has loved me since a long time, and I have refused to accede to his desires, nor did I listen to him, though the saliva was dried up in his mouth by his supplications; and in spite of the large expenses he had gone to in order to gain my favour I have always answered him that I should not consent, and now, O my mother, I am afraid that he might call to God to curse me.'

'Tell me how to know this man,' said the old woman, 'for fear that you might become like this animal.'

'But how will you be able to find him, and whom could I send to him?'

The old woman answered, 'Me, daughter of mine! I shall render you this service, and find him.'

'Make haste, O my mother, and see him before he conjures God against me.'

'I shall find him still this day,' answered the old woman, 'and, please God, you shall meet him tomorrow.'

With this, the old woman took her leave, went on the same day to the man who had made her his confidant, and told him of the meeting arranged for next day.

So the next day the mistress of the house went to the old woman, for they had agreed that the rendezvous should take place there. When she arrived at the house she waited for some time, but the lover did not come. No doubt he had been prevented from making his appearance by some matter of importance.

The old woman, reflecting upon this mischance, thought to herself, 'There is no might nor power but in God, the Great.' Looking at the woman, she saw that she was agitated, and it was apparent that she wanted coition hotly. She got more and more restless, and presently asked, 'Why does he not come?' The old woman made answer, 'O my daughter, some serious affair must have interfered. But I shall help you under these circumstances.' She then went to look for the young man. But it was to no purpose, as she could not find out anything about him.

Still continuing her search, the old woman was thinking, 'This woman is eagerly coveting a man. Why not try today another, who might calm her ardour? Tomorrow I shall find the right one.' As she was thus walking she met a young man of very pleasing exterior. She saw, at once, that he was a fit lover, and she spoke to him: 'O my son, if I were to set you in connection with a lady, beautiful, graceful and perfect, would you make love to her?' 'If your words are truth, I would give you this golden dinar!' said he. The old woman, quite enchanted, took the money, and conducted him to her house.

Now, it so happened that this man was the husband of the lady, which the old woman did not know. And the way she found it out was this: She went first into the house and said to the lady, 'I have not been able to find your lover; but I have brought you somebody to quench your fire for today. We will save the other for tomorrow. God has inspired me to do so.'

The lady then went to the window to take a look at him and recognized her husband, just on the point of entering the house. She did not hesitate, but hastily donning her *melahfa,* she went straight to meet him, and striking him in the face, she exclaimed, 'O! enemy of God and of yourself, what are you doing here? You surely came with the intention to commit adultery. I have been suspecting you for a long time, and waited here every day, while I was sending out the old woman to inveigle you to come in. This day I have found you out, and denial is of no use. And you always told me that you were not a rake! I shall demand a divorce this very day, now I know your conduct!'

98

The husband, believing that his wife spoke the truth, remained silent and abashed.

Learn from this the deceitfulness of woman, and what she is capable of.

Story of the Lover against his Will

A story is told of a certain woman who was desperately in love with one of her neighbours, whose virtue and piety were well known. She declared to him her passion; but, finding all her advances constantly repulsed, in spite of all her wiles, she resolved to have her satisfaction nevertheless, and this is the way she went to work her purpose:

One evening she apprised her negress that she intended to set a snare for that man, and the negress, by her order, left the street door open; then, in the middle of the night, she called the negress and gave her the following instructions: 'Go and knock with this stone at our street door as hard as you can, without taking any notice of the cries which I shall utter, or the noise I make; as soon as you hear the neighbour opening his door, come back and knock the same way at the inner door. Take care that he does not see you, and come in at once if you observe somebody coming.' The negress executed this order punctually.

Now, the neighbour was by nature a compassionate man, always disposed to assist people in distress, and his help was never asked in vain. On hearing the noise of the blows struck at the door and the cries of his neighbour, he asked his wife what this might mean, and she replied, 'It is our neighbour, who is attacked in her house by thieves.' He went in great haste to her aid; but scarcely had he entered when the negress closed the door upon him. The woman seized him, and uttered loud screams. He protested, but the mistress of the house put this condition before him. 'If you do not consent to do with me so and so, I shall tell that you have come in here to violate me, and hence all this noise.' 'The will of God be done!' said the man, 'nobody can go against Him, nor escape from His might.' He then tried sundry subterfuges in order to escape, but in vain, for the mistress of the house recommenced to scream and make a row. He saw that his reputation would be compromised if he continued his resistance, and surrendered, saying, 'Save me, and I am ready to satisfy you!' 'Go into this chamber and close the door behind you,' said the lady of the house, 'if you want to leave this house with honour, and do not attempt escape unless you wish those people to know that you are the author of all this commotion.' When he saw how determined she was to have her way, he did as she had told him. She, on her part, went out to the neighbours that had come to help her, and giving them some kind of explanation, dismissed them.

Left alone, she shut the doors and returned to her unwilling lover. She kept him in sequestration for a whole week, and only set him free after she had completely drained him.

Learn from this the deceitfulness of women, and what they are capable of.

A Larceny of Love

The following story is told of two women who inhabited the same house. The husband of one of them had a member long, thick and hard; while the husband of the other had, on the contrary, that organ little, insignificant and soft. The first one rose always pleasant and smiling; the other one got up in the morning in tears and vexation.

One day the two women were together, and spoke of their husbands.

The first one said, 'I live in the greatest happiness. My bed is a couch of bliss. When my husband and I are together in it it is the witness of our supreme pleasure; of our kisses and embraces, of our joys and amorous sighs. When my husband's member is in my vulva it stops it up completely; it stretches itself out until it touches the bottom of my vagina, and it does not take its leave until it has visited every corner—threshold, vestibule, ceiling and centre. When the crisis arrives it takes its position in the very centre of the vagina, which it floods with tears. It is in this way we quench our fire and appease our passion.'

The second answered, 'I live in the greatest grief; our bed is a bed of misery, and our coition is a union of fatigue and trouble, of hate and malediction. When my husband's member enters my vulva there is a space left open, and it is so short it cannot touch the bottom. When it is in erection it is twisted all ways, and cannot procure any pleasure. Feeble and meagre, it can scarcely ejaculate a drop, and its service cannot afford pleasure to any woman.'

Such was the almost daily conversation which the two women had together.

It happened, however, that the woman who had so much cause for complaint thought in her heart how delightful it would be to commit adultery with the other one's husband. She thought to herself, 'It must be brought about, if only for once.' Then she watched her opportunity until her husband had to be absent.

In the evening she made preparation to get her project carried

100

out, and perfumed herself with sweet scents and essences. When the night was advanced to about a third of its duration, she noiselessly entered the chamber in which the other woman and her husband were sleeping, and groped her way to their couch. Finding that there was a free space between them, she slipped in. There was scant room, but each of the spouses thought it was the pressure of the other, and gave way a little; and so she contrived to glide between them. She then quietly waited until the other woman was in a profound sleep, and then, approaching the husband, she brought her flesh in contact with his. He awoke, and smelling the perfumed odours which she exhaled, he was in erection at once. He drew her towards him, but she said, in a low voice, 'Let me go to sleep!' He answered, 'Be quiet, and let me do! The children will not hear anything!' She then pressed close up to him, so as to get him farther away from his wife, and said, 'Do as you like, but do not awaken the children, who are close by.' She took these precautions for fear that his wife should wake up.

The man, however, roused by the odour of the perfumes, drew her ardently towards himself. She was plump and mellow, and her vulva projecting. He mounted upon her and said, 'Take it (the member) in your hand, as usual!' She took it, and was astonished at its size and magnificence, then introduced it into her vulva.

The man, however, observed that his member had been taken in entirely, which he had never been able to do with his wife. The woman, on her part, found that she had never received such a benefit from her husband.

The man was quite surprised. He worked his will upon her a second and third time, but his astonishment only increased. At last he got off her, and stretched himself along her side.

As soon as the woman found that he was asleep, she slipped out, left the chamber, and returned to her own.

In the morning, the husband, on rising, said to his wife, 'Your embraces have never seemed so sweet to me as last night, and I never breathed such sweet perfumes as those you exhaled.' 'What embraces and what perfumes are you speaking of?' asked the wife. 'I have not a particle of perfume in the house.' She assured him that he must have been dreaming.

Appreciate, after this, the deceitfulness of women, and what they are capable of.

Story of the Woman with Two Husbands

It is related that a man, after having lived for some time in a country to which he had gone, became desirous of getting married.

He addressed himself to an old woman who had experience in such matters, asking her whether she could find him a wife, and who replied, 'I can find you a girl gifted with great beauty, and perfect in shape and comeliness. She will surely suit you, for, besides, she is virtuous and pure. Only mark, her business occupies her all the day, but during the night she will be yours completely. It is for this reason she keeps herself reserved, as a husband might not agree to this.'

The man replied, 'This girl need not be afraid. I, too, am not at liberty during the day, and I only want her for the night.'

He then asked her in marriage. The old woman brought her to him, and he liked her. From that time they lived together, observing the conditions under which they had come together.

This man had an intimate friend whom he introduced to the old woman who had arranged his marriage, and which friend had requested the man to ask her to do him the same service. 'This is a very easy matter,' she said. 'I know a girl of great beauty, who will dissipate your heaviest troubles. Only the business she is carrying on keeps her at work all night, but she will be with your friend all day long.' 'This shall be no hindrance,' replied the friend. She then brought the young girl to him. He was well pleased with her, and married her.

But before long the two friends found out that the two wives which the old harridan had procured for them were only one woman.

Appreciate, after this, the deceitfulness of women, and what they are capable of.

Story of Bahia

It is related that a married woman of the name of Bahia had a lover whose relations to her were soon a mystery to no one, for which reason she had to leave him. Her absence affected him to such a degree that he fell ill.

One day he went to see one of his friends, and said to him, 'Oh, my brother! an ungovernable desire has seized me, and I can wait no more. Could you accompany me on a visit I am going to pay to Bahia, the well-beloved of my heart?' The friend declared himself willing.

The next day they mounted their horses; and after a journey of two days, they arrived near the place where Bahia dwelt. The lover said to his friend, 'Go and see the people that live about here, but take good care not to divulge our intentions, and try in particular to find the servant-girl of Bahia, to whom you can say that I am here, and whom you will charge with the message to her mistress that I would like to see her.

The friend went, met the servant, and told her all that was necessary. She went at once to Bahia, and repeated to her what she had been told.

Bahia sent to the friend the message, 'Inform him who sent you that the meeting will take place tonight, near such and such a tree, at such and such an hour.'

At the hour that had been fixed, the two friends were near to the tree. They had not to wait long for Bahia. As soon as her lover saw her coming, he rushed to meet her, kissed her, pressed her to his heart, and they began to embrace and caress each other.

The lover said to her, 'O Bahia, is there no way to enable us to pass the night together without rousing the suspicions of your husband?' She answered, 'Oh, before God! if it will give you pleasure, the means to contrive this are not wanting. Your friend here, is he devoted to you, and intelligent?' He answered, 'Yes.' She then rose, took off her garments, and handed them to the friend, who gave her his, in which she then dressed herself; then she made the friend put on her clothes, and gave the following explanations: 'Go to my house and lie down in my bed. After a third part of the night is passed, my husband will come to you and ask you for the pot into which they milk the camels. Then he will go and return with the pot filled with milk, and say to you, "Here is the pot!" Then take it out of his hands. After that, you will not see anything more of him till the morning.'

The friend went, observed all these recommendations, and when the husband returned with the pot full of milk he did not take it out of his hands until he had said, 'Here is the pot!' Unfortunately the vase fell upon the ground and was broken. The husband, in the belief that he was speaking to his wife, exclaimed, 'What have you been thinking of?' and beat him with it till it broke; then took another, and continued to batter him stroke on stroke enough to break his back. The mother and sister of Bahia came running to the spot to tear her from his hands. He had fainted. Luckily they succeeded in getting the husband away.

The mother of Bahia soon came back, and talked to him so long that he was fairly sick of her talk; but he could do nothing but be silent and weep. At last she finished, saying, 'Have confidence in God, and obey your husband. As for your lover, he cannot come now to see and console you, but I will send your sister to keep you company.' And she she went away.

She did send, indeed, the sister of Bahia, who began to console her and curse him who had beaten her. He felt his heart warming towards her, for he had seen that she was of resplendent beauty, endowed with all perfections, and like the full moon in the night. He placed his hand over her mouth, so as to prevent her from speaking, and said to her, 'O, lady! I am not what you think. Your sister Bahia is at present with her lover, and I have run into danger to do her a service. Will you not take me under your protection? If you denounce me, your sister will be covered with shame; as for me, I have done my part, but may the evil fall back upon you!'

The young girl then began to tremble like a leaf, in thinking of the consequences of her sister's doings, and then beginning to laugh, surrendered herself to the friend who proved himself so true. They passed the remainder of the night in bliss, kisses, embraces, and mutual enjoyment. He found her the best of the best. In her arms he forgot the beating he had received, and they did not cease to play, toy, and make love till daybreak.

He then returned to his companion. Bahia asked him how he had fared, and he said to her, 'Ask your sister. By my faith! she knows it all! Only know, that we have passed the night in mutual pleasures, kissing and enjoying ourselves until now.'

Then they changed clothes again, each one taking his own, and the friend told Bahia all the particulars of what had happened to him.

Appreciate, after this, the deceitfulness of women, and what they are capable of.

The Story of the Expert Duped by a Woman

A story is told of a man who had studied all the ruses and all the stratagems invented by women for the deception of men, and pretended that no woman could dupe him.

A woman of great beauty, and full of charms, got to hear of his conceit. She, therefore, prepared for him a collation, in which several kinds of wine figured, and nothing was wanting in the way of rare and choice viands. Then she invited him to come and see her. As she was famed for her great beauty and the rare perfection of her person, she had roused his desires, and he made haste to avail himself of her invitation.

She was dressed in her finest garments, and exhaled the choicest perfumes, and assuredly whoever had thus seen her would have been troubled in his mind. And thus, when he was admitted into her presence, he was fascinated by her charms, and plunged into admiration by her marvellous beauty.

This woman, however, appeared to be preoccupied on account of her husband, and allowed it to be seen that she was afraid of his coming back from one minute to another. It must be mentioned that this husband was very proud, very jealous, and very violent, and would not have hesitated to shed the blood of anyone whom he would have found prowling about his house. What would he have done, and, with much more reason, to the man whom he might have found inside!

While the lady and he, who flattered himself that he should possess her, were amusing themselves, a knock at the house-door filled the lover with fear, particularly when the lady cried, 'This is my husband, returning.' All in a tremble, she hid him in a closet, which was in the room, shut the door upon him, and left the key in; then she opened the house-door.

Her husband, for it was he, saw, on entering, the wine and all the preparations that had been made. Surprised, he asked what this meant. 'It means what you see,' she answered. 'But for whom is all this?' he asked.

'It is for my lover whom I have here.'

'And where is he?'

'In this closet,' she said, pointing with her finger to the place where the sufferer was confined.

At these words the husband started. He rose and went to the closet, but found it locked. 'Where is the key?' he said. She answered, 'Here!' throwing it to him. But as he was putting it into the lock she burst out laughing uproariously. He turned towards her, and said, 'What are you laughing at?' I laugh,' she answered, 'at the weakness of your judgment, and your want of reason and reflection. Oh, you man without sense, do you think that if I had in reality a lover, and had admitted him into this room, I should have told you that he was here and where he was hidden? That is certainly not likely. I had no other thought than to offer you a collation on your return, and wanted only to have a joke with you in doing as I did. If I had had a lover I should certainly not have made you my confidant.'

The husband left the key in the lock of the closet without having turned it, returned to the table, and said, 'True! I rose; but I have not the slightest doubt about the sincerity of your words.' Then they ate and drank together, and made love.

The man in the closet had to stop there until the husband went out. Then the lady went to set him free, and found him quite undone and in a bad state. When he came out, after having escaped an eminent peril, she said to him, 'Well, you wiseacre, who know so well the stratagems of women, of all those you know, is there one to equal this?' He made answer, 'I am now convinced that your stratagems are countless.'

Appreciate after this the deceits of women, and what they are capable of.

Story of the Lover who was surprised by the Unexpected Arrival of the Husband

It is related that a woman who was married to a violent and brutal man, having her lover with her on the unexpected arrival of her husband, had only just time to hide him under the bed. She was compelled to let him remain in this dangerous and unpleasant position, knowing of no expedient which might enable him to leave the house. In her restlessness she went to and fro, and having gone to the street-door, one of her neighbours, a woman, saw that she was in trouble, and asked her the reason of it. She told her what had happened. The other one then said, 'Return into the house. I will charge myself with the safety of your lover, and I promise you that he shall come out unharmed.' Then the woman re-entered her house.

Her neighbour was not long in joining her, and together they prepared the meal, and then they all sat down to eat and drink. The woman sat facing her husband, and the neighbour opposite the bed. The latter began to tell stories and anecdotes about the tricks of women; and the lover under the bed heard all that was going on.

Pursuing her tales, the neighbour told the following one: 'A married woman had a lover, whom she loved tenderly, and by whom she was equally loved. One day the lover came to see her in the absence of her husband. But the latter happened to return home unexpectedly just as they were together. The woman, knowing of no better place, hid her lover under the bed, then sat down by her husband, who was taking some refreshment, and joked and played with him. Amongst other playful games, she covered her husband's eyes with a napkin, and her lover took this opportunity to come out from under the bed and escape unobserved.'

The wife understood at once how to profit by this tale; taking a napkin and covering the eyes of her husband with it, she said, 'Then it was by means of this ruse that the lover was helped out of his dilemma.' And the lover, taking the opportunity, succeeded in making good his escape unobserved by the husband. Unconscious of what had happened this latter laughed at the story, and his merriment was still increased by the last words of his wife and by her action.

Appreciate after this the deceitfulness of women, and what they are capable of.

106

CHAPTER 12

Concerning Sundry Observations useful to know for Men and Women

Know, O Vizir (to whom God be good!), that the information contained in this chapter is of the greatest utility, and it is only in this book that such can be found. Assuredly to know things is better than to be ignorant of them. Knowledge may be bad, but ignorance is still more so.

The knowledge in question concerns matters unknown to you, and relating to women.

There was once a woman, named Moârbeda, who was considered to be the most knowing and wisest person of her time. She was a philosopher. One day various queries were put to her, and among them the following, which I shall give here, with her answers.

'In what part of a woman's body does her mind reside?'

'Between her thighs.'

'And where her enjoyment?'

'In the same place.'

'And where the love of men and the hatred of them?'

'In the vulva,' she said; adding, 'to the man whom we love we give our vulva, and we refuse it to him we hate. We share our property with the man we love, and are content with whatever little he may be able to bring to us; if he has no fortune, we take him as he is. But, on the other hand, we keep at a distance him whom we hate, were he to offer us wealth and riches.'

'Where, in a woman, are located knowledge, love and taste?'

'In the eye, the heart, and the vulva.'

When asked for explanations on this subject, she replied: 'Knowledge dwells in the eye, for it is the woman's eye that appreciates the beauty of form and of appearance. By the medium of this organ love penetrates into the heart and dwells in it, and enslaves it. A woman in love pursues the object of her love, and lays snares for it. If she succeed, there will be an encounter between the beloved one and her vulva. The vulva tastes him and then knows his sweet or bitter flavour. It is, in fact, the vulva which knows how to distinguish by tasting the good from the bad.'

'Which virile members are preferred by women? What women are most eager for coitus, and which are those who detest it? Which are the men preferred by women, and which are those whom they abominate?'

She answered, 'Not all women have the same conformation of vulva, and they also differ in their manner of making love, and in their love for and their aversion to things. The same disparities exist in men, both with regard to their organs and their tastes. A woman of plump form and with a shallow uterus will look out for a member which is both short and thick, which will completely fill her vagina, without touching the bottom of it; a long and large member would not suit her. A woman with a deep lying uterus, and consequently a long vagina, only yearns for a member which is long and thick and of ample proportions, and thus fills her vagina in its whole extension; she will despise the man with a small and slender member for he could never satisfy her in coition.

'The following distinctions exist in the temperaments of women: the bilious, the melancholy, the sanguine, the phlegmatic, and the mixed. Those with a bilious or melancholy temperament are not much given to coitus, and like it only with men of the same disposition. Those who are sanguine or phlegmatic love coition to excess, and if they encounter a member, they would never let it leave their vulva if they could help it. With these also it is only men of their own temperament who can satisfy them, and if such a woman were married to a bilious or melancholy man, they would lead a sorry life together. As regards mixed temperaments, they exhibit neither a marked predilection for, nor aversion against coitus.

'It has been observed that under all circumstances little women love coitus more and evince a stronger affection for the virile member than women of a large size. Only long and vigorous members suit them; in them they find the delight of their existence and of their couch.

'There are also women who love the coitus only on the edge of their vulva, and when a man lying upon them wants to get his member into the vagina, they take it out with the hand and place its gland between the lips of the vulva.'

I have every reason to believe that this is only the case with young girls or with women not used to men. I pray God to preserve us from such, or from women for whom it is a matter of impossibility to give themselves up to men.

'There are women who will do their husband's behests, and

108

will satisfy them and give them voluptuous pleasure by coition, only if compelled by blows and ill-treatment. Some people ascribe this conduct to the aversion they feel either against coition or against the husband; but this is not so; it is simply a question of temperament and character.

'There are also women who do not care for coition because all their ideas turn upon the grandeurs, personal honours, ambitious hopes, or business-cares of the world. With others this indifference springs, as it may be, from purity of the heart, or from jealousy, or from a pronounced tendency of their souls towards another world, or lastly from past violent sorrows. Furthermore, the pleasures which they feel in coition depend not alone upon the size of the member, but also upon the particular conformation of their own natural parts. Amongst those the vulva called from its form *el mortebâ,* the square one, and *el mortafâ,* the projecting, is remarkable. This vulva has the peculiarity of projecting all round when the woman is standing up and closes her thighs. It burns for the coitus, its slit is narrow, and it is also called *el ķeulihimi,* the pressed one. The woman who has such a one likes only large members, and they must not let her wait long for the crisis. But this is a general characteristic of women.

'As to the desire of men for coition, I must say that they also are addicted to it more or less according to their different temperaments, five in number, like the women's with the difference that the hankering of the woman after the member is stronger than that of the man after the vulva.'

'What are the faults of women?' Moârbeda replied to this question, 'The worst of women is she who immediately cries out aloud as soon as her husband wants to touch the smallest amount of her property for his necessities. In the same line stands she who divulges matters which her husband wants to be kept secret.'

'Are there any more?' she is asked. She adds, 'The woman of a jealous disposition and the woman who raises her voice so as to drown that of her husband; she who disseminates scandal; the woman that scowls; the one who is always burning to let men see her beauty, and cannot stay at home; and with respect to this last let me add that a woman who laughs much, and is constantly seen at the street door, may be taken to be an arrant prostitute.

'Bad also are those women who mind other people's affairs; those who are always complaining; those who steal things belonging to their husbands; those of a disagreeable and imperious temper; those who are not grateful for kindnesses received; those that will not share the conjugal couch, or who incommode their husbands by the uncomfortable positions they take in it; those who are inclined to deceit, treachery, calumny and ruse.

'Then there are still women who are unlucky in whatever they undertake; those who are always inclined to blame and censure; those who invite their husbands to fulfil their conjugal duty only when it is convenient for them; those that make noises in bed; and lastly those who are shameless, without intelligence, tattlers and curious.

'Here you have the worst specimens amongst women.'

CHAPTER 13

Concerning the Causes of Enjoyment in the Act of Generation

Know, O Vizir (to whom God be good!), that the causes which tend to develop the passion for coition are six in number: the fire of an ardent love, the superabundance of sperm, the proximity of the loved person whose possession is eagerly desired, the beauty of the face, exciting viands, and contact.

Know also, that the causes of the pleasure in cohabitation, and the conditions of enjoyment are numerous, but that the principal and best ones are: the heat of the vulva; the narrowness, dryness, and sweet exhalation of the same. If any one of these conditions is absent, there is at the same time something wanting in the voluptuous enjoyment. But if the vagina unites the required qualifications, the enjoyment is complete. In fact, a moist vulva relaxes the nerves, a cold one robs the member of all its vigour, and bad exhalations from the vagina detract greatly from the pleasure, as is also the case if the latter is very wide.

The acme of enjoyment, which is produced by the abundance and impetuous ejaculation of the sperm, depends upon one circumstance, and this is, that the vulva is furnished with a suction-pump (orifice of the uterus), which will clasp the virile member, and suck up the sperm with an irresistible force. The member once seized by the orifice, the lover is powerless to retain the sperm, for the orifice will not relax its hold until it has extracted every drop of the sperm, and certainly if the crisis arrives before this gripping of the gland takes place, the pleasure of the ejaculation will not be complete.

Know that there are eight things which give strength to and favour the ejaculation. These are: bodily health, the absence of all care and worry, an unembarrassed mind, natural gaiety of spirit, good nourishment, wealth, the variety of the faces of women, and the variety of their complexions.

A savant of the name of Djelinouss has said: 'He who feels that he is weak for coition should drink before going to bed a glassful of very thick honey and eat twenty almonds and one hundred grains of the pine tree. He must follow this *régime* for three days.'

The virile member, rubbed with ass's milk, will become uncommonly strong and vigorous.

Green peas, boiled carefully with onions, and powdered with cinnamon, ginger and cardamoms, well pounded, create for the consumer considerable amorous passion and strength in coitus.

CHAPTER 14

Description of the Uterus of Sterile Women, and Treatment of the Same

Know, O Vizir (God be good to you!), that wise physicians have plunged into this sea of difficulties to very little purpose. Each one has looked at the matter from his own point of view, and in the end the question has been left in the dark.

Amongst the causes which determine the sterility of women may be taken the obstruction in the uterus by clots of blood, the accumulation of water, the want of or defective sperm of the man, organic malformation of the parts of the latter, internal defects in the uterus, stagnation of the courses and the corruption of the menstrual fluid, and the habitual presence of wind in the uterus. Other savants attribute the sterility of women to the action of spirits and spells. Sterility is common in women who are very corpulent, so that their uterus gets compressed and cannot conceive, not being able to take up the sperm, especially if the husband's member is short and his testicles are very fat; in such a case the act of copulation can only be imperfectly completed.

One of the remedies against sterility consists of the marrow from the hump of a camel, which the woman spreads on a piece of linen, and rubs her sexual parts with it, after having been purified subsequently to her courses.

CHAPTER 15

Concerning Medicines which Provoke Abortion

Know, O Vizir (God be good to you!) that the medicines which will bring on abortion, and the ejection of the foetus, are innumerable. But I shall speak of those to you which I have proved, and therefore acknowledge as good, so that everybody may learn what may benefit and what may do harm.

I shall in the first place speak of the madder-root. A small quantity of this substance freshly gathered, or even dried, but in the latter case bruised and moistened at the time when it is to be used, vitiates the virile sperm or kills the foetus, bringing abortion on and provoking menstruation when introduced in the woman's vagina.

The man who at the moment of copulation coats his member with tar, deprives his sperm of its generative faculty. This is the most powerful of all applications.

The woman who drinks the weight of a *mitskal* of laurel water, with a little pepper, will cause her courses to flow again.

The woman who drinks an infusion of coarse cinnamon mixed with red myrrh, and then introduces into her vagina a plug of wool saturated with the mixture, kills the foetus and provokes its expulsion, with the will of God the Highest!

All the above enumerated medicines are efficacious and their effect is certain.

CHAPTER 16

Concerning the Causes of Impotence in Men

Know, O Vizir (God be good to you!) that there are men whose sperm is vitiated by the inborn coldness of their nature, by diseases of their organs, by purulent discharges, and by fevers. There are also men with the urinary canal in their verge deviating owing to a downward curve; the result of such conformation is that the seminal liquid cannot be ejected in a straight direction, but falls downwards.

Other men have the member too short and too small to reach the neck of the matrix, or their bladder is ulcerated, or they are affected by other infirmities, which prevent them from coition.

Finally, there are men who arrive quicker at the crisis than women, in consequence of which the two emissions are not simultaneous; there is in such cases no conception.

All these circumstances serve to explain the absence of conception in women; but the principal cause of all is the shortness of the virile member.

As another cause of impotence may be regarded the sudden transmission from hot to cold, and vice versa, and a great number of analogous reasons.

Men whose impotence is due either to the corruption of their sperm owing to their cold nature, or to maladies of the organs, or to discharges or fevers and similar ills, or to their excessive promptness in ejaculation, can be cured. They should eat stimulant pastry containing honey, ginger, pyrether, syrup of vinegar, hellebore, garlic, cinnamon, nutmeg, cardamoms, sparrows tongues, Chinese cinnamon, long pepper, and other spices. They will be cured by using them.

As to the other afflictions which we have indicated—the curvature of the urethra, the small dimensions of the virile member, ulcers on the bladder, and the other infirmities which are adverse to coition—God only can cure them.

CHAPTER 17

Undoing of Aiguillettes
(Impotence for a Time)

Know, O Vizir (God be good to you!), that impotence arises from three causes:

Firstly, from the tying of aiguillettes.

Secondly, from a feeble and relaxed constitution.

And thirdly, from too premature ejaculation.

To cure the tying of aiguillettes you must take *galanga,* cinnamon, cloves, cachou, nutmeg, cubebs, sparrow-wort, pepper, thistle, cardamoms, pyrether, laurel-seed, and gilly-flowers.

The man whose ejaculation is too precipitate must take nutmeg and incense (*oliban*) mixed together with honey.

If the impotence arises from weakness, the following ingredients are to be taken in honey: pyrether, nettle-seed, a little spurge, ginger, cinnamon of Mecca, and cardamom.

The impossibility of coitus, owing to absense of stiffness in the member, is also due to other causes. It will happen, for instance, that a man with his verge in erection will find it getting flaccid just when he is on the point of introducing it. He thinks this is impotence, while it is simply the result, may be, of an exaggerated respect for the woman, may be of a misplaced bashfulness, may be because one has observed something disagreeable, or on account of and unpleasant odour; finally, owing to a feeling of jealousy, inspired by the reflection that the woman is no longer a virgin, and has served the pleasures of other men.

CHAPTER 18

Prescriptions for Increasing the Dimensions
of Small members and for making them Splendid

Know, O Vizir (God be good to you!), that this chapter which treats of the size of the virile member, is of the first importance both for men and women. For the men, because from a good-sized and vigorous member there springs the affection and love of women; for the women, because it is by such members that their amorous passions are appeased, and the greatest pleasure is procured for them. This is evident from the fact that many men, solely by reason of their insignificant members, are, as far as coition is concerned, objects of aversion to women, who likewise entertain the same sentiment with regard to those whose members are soft, nerveless, and relaxed. Their whole happiness consists in the use of robust and strong members.

A man, therefore, with a small member, who wants to make it grand or fortify it for the coitus, must rub it before copulation with tepid water, until it gets red and extended by the blood flowing into it, in consequence of the heat; he must then anoint it with a mixture of honey and ginger, rubbing it in sedulously. Then let him join the woman; he will procure for her such pleasure that she objects to him getting off her again.

Another remedy consists in a compound made of a moderate quantity of pepper, lavender, galanga, and musk, reduced to powder, sifted, and mixed up with honey and preserved ginger. The member, after having been first washed in warm water, is then vigorously rubbed with the mixture; it will then grow large and brawny, and afford to the woman a marvellous feeling of voluptuousness.

A third remedy is the following: wash the member in warm water until it becomes red, and enters into erection. Then take a piece of soft leather, upon which spread hot pitch, and envelope the member with it. It will not be long before the member raises its head, trembling with passion.

A fourth remedy is based upon the use made of leeches, but

only of such as live in water (*sic*). You put as many of them into a bottle as can be got in, and fill it up with oil. Then expose the bottle to the sun, until the heat of the same has effected a complete mixture. With the fluid thus obtained the member is to be rubbed several consecutive days, and it will, by being thus treated, become of a good size and of full dimensions.

For another procedure I will here note the use of an ass's member. Procure one and boil it, with onions and a large quantity of corn. With this dish feed fowls, which you eat afterwards.

Another way is to bruise leeches with oil, and rub the verge with this ointment; or the leeches may be put into a bottle, and buried in a warm dunghill until they are dissolved and form a sort of liniment, which is used for repeatedly anointing the member. The member is certain to greatly benefit by this.

The efficacy of all these remedies is well known, and I have tested them.

CHAPTER 19

Of things that take away the Bad Smell from the Armpits and Sexual Parts of Women and Contract the Latter

Know, O Vizir (God be good to you!), that bad exhalations from the vulva and of the armpits are, as also a wide vagina, the greatest of evils.

If a woman wants this bad odour to disappear she must pound red myrrh, then sift it, and knead this powder with myrtle-water, and rub her sexual parts with this wash. All disagreeable emanation will disappear from her vulva.

Another remedy is obtained by pounding lavender, and kneading it afterwards with musk-rose-water. Saturate a piece of woolen-stuff with it, and rub the vulva with the same until it is hot. The bad smell will be removed by this.

If a woman intends to contract her vagina, she has only to dissolve alum in water, and wash her sexual parts with the solution, which may be made still more efficacious by the addition of a little bark of the walnut-tree, the latter substance being very astringent.

Another remedy to be mentioned is the following, which is well known for its efficacy: Boil well in water carobs (locusts), freed from their kernels, and bark of the pomegranate tree. The woman takes a sitz bath in the decoction thus obtained, and which must be as hot as she can bear it; when the bath gets cold, it must be warmed and used again, and this immersion is to be repeated several times. The same result may be obtained by fumigating the vulva with cow-dung.

To do away with the bad smell of the armpits, one takes antimony and mastic, which are to be pounded together, and put with water into an earthen vase. The mixture is then rubbed against the sides of the vase until it turns red; when it is ready for use, rub it into the armpits, and the bad smell will be removed. It must be used repeatedly, until a radical cure is effected.

The same result may be arrived at by pounding together antimony (*hadida*) and mastic, setting the mixture afterwards onto a stove over a low fire, until it is of the consistency of bread, and rubbing the residue with a stone until the pellicle, which will have formed, is removed. Then rub it into the armpits, and you may be sure that the bad smell will soon be gone.

CHAPTER 20

*Instructions with regard to Pregnancy and
how the Gender of the Child that is to be
Born may be known—that is to say,
Knowledge of the Sex of the Foetus*

Know, O Vizir (God be good to you!), that the certain indications of pregnancy are the following: the dryness of the vulva immediately after coitus, the inclination to stretch herself, accesses of somnolency, heavy and profound sleep, the frequent contraction of the opening of the vulva to such an extent that not even a *meroud* could penetrate, the nipples of the breast become darker, and lastly, the most certain of all marks is the cessation of menstruation.

If the woman remains always in good health from the time that her pregnancy is certain, if she preserves the good looks of her face and a clear complexion, if she does not become freckled, then it may be taken as a sign that the child will be a boy.

The red colour of the nipples also points to a child of the male sex. The strong development of the breasts, and bleeding from the nose, if it comes from the right nostril, are signs of the same purport.

The signs pointing to the conception of a child of the female sex are numerous. I will name them here: frequent indisposition during pregnancy, pale complexion, spots and freckles, pains in the matrix, frequent nightmares, blackness of the nipples, a heavy feeling on the left side, nasal hemorrhage on the same side.

If there is any doubt about the pregnancy, let the woman drink, on going to bed, honey-water, and if then she has a feeling of heaviness in the abdomen, it is a proof that she is with child. If the right side feels heavier than the left one, it will be a boy. If the breasts are swelling with milk, this is similarly a sign that the child she is bearing will be of the male sex.

I have received this information from savants, and all the indications are positive and tested.

CHAPTER 21

Forming the Conclusion of this Work, and Treating of the Good Effects of the Deglutition of Eggs as Favourable to the Coitus

Know, O Vizir (God be good to you!), that this chapter contains the most useful instructions—how to increase the intensity of the coitus—and that the latter part is profitable to read for an old man as well as for the man in his best years and for the young man.

He who makes it a practice to eat every day fasting the yolks of eggs, without the white part, will find in this aliment an energetic stimulant towards coitus.

He who for several days makes his meals upon eggs boiled with myrrh, coarse cinnamon, and pepper, will find his vigour with respect to coition and erections greatly increased.

A man who wishes to copulate during a whole night, and whose desire, having come on suddenly, will not allow him to prepare himself and follow the regimen just mentioned, must get a great number of eggs, and fry them with fresh fat and butter; when done he immerses them in honey. He must then eat of them as much as possible with a little bread, and for the whole night his member will not give him any rest.

On this subject the following verses have been composed:

The member of Abou el Heïloukh has remained erect
For thirty days without a break, because he did eat onions.
Abou el Heïdja has deflowered in one night
Once eighty virgins, and he did not eat or drink between,
Because he'd surfeited himself first with chick-peas,
And had drunk camel's milk with honey mixed.
Mimoun, the negro, never ceased to spend his sperm, while he
For fifty days with a truce the game was working.
How proud he was to finish such a task!
For ten days more he worked it, not was he yet surfeited,
But all this time he ate but yolk of eggs and bread.

122

The deeds of Abou el Heïloukh, Abou el Heïdja and Mimoun, just cited, have been justly praised, and their history is truly marvellous. So I will make you acquainted with it, please God, and thus complete the signal services which this work is designed to render to humanity.

The History of Zohra

The *Cheikh,* the protector of religion (God, the Highest, be good to him!) records, that there lived once in remote antiquity an illustrious King, who had numerous armies and immense riches.

This King had seven daughters remarkable for their beauty and perfections.

The Kings of the time wanted them in marriage, but they refused to be married. They wore men's clothing, rode on magnificent horses covered with gold-embroidered trappings, knew how to handle the sword and the spear, and bore men down in single combat. Each of them possessed a splendid palace.

Zohra, the youngest, was at the same time the most intelligent and judicious.

She was passionately fond of the chase, and one day as she was riding through the fields she met on her way a cavalier. He could not help admiring secretly her hand, the gracefulness of her waist, and the amorous expression of her eyes. His heart was seized with a violent love.

The following conversation took place between them:

The Cavalier: 'Is your heart insensible for friendship?'

Zohra: 'It is not proper for a man to feel friendship for a woman; for if their hearts once incline towards each other, libidinous desires will soon invade them, and with Satan enticing them to do wrong, their fall is soon known by everyone.'

The Cavalier: 'It is not so, when the affection is true and their intercourse pure without infidelity or treachery.'

Zohra: 'If a woman gives way to the affection she feels for a man, she becomes an object of slander and of general contempt, whence nothing arises but trouble and regrets.'

The Cavalier: 'But our love will remain secret, and in this retired spot, which may serve us as our place of meeting, we shall have intercourse together unknown to all.'

Zohra: 'That may not be. Besides, it could not so easily be done, we should soon be suspected.'

The Cavalier: 'But love, love is the source of life. The happiness, that is, the meeting, the embraces, the caresses of lovers.'

Zohra: 'These words are impregnated with love, and your smile is seductive; but you would do better to refrain from similar conversation.'

The Cavalier: 'Your word is emerald and your counsels are sincere. But love has now taken root in my heart, and no one is able to tear it out. If you drive me from you I shall assuredly die.'

Zohra: 'For all that you must return to your place and I to mine. If it pleases God we shall meet again.'

They then separated, bidding each other adieu.

The cavalier's name was Abou el Heïdja. His father, Kheiroun, was a great merchant and immensely rich, whose habitation stood isolated beyond the estate of the princess, a day's journey distant from her castle, Abou el Heïdja returned home, could not rest, and when the night fell, took a black turban, mounted his horse, and, accompanied by his favourite negro, Mimoun, he rode away secretly under the cover of night.

They travelled all night without stopping until the dawn came upon them in sight of Zohra's castle. They then entered with their horses into a cavern which they found there.

Abou el Heïdja went in the direction of the castle; he found it surrounded by a very high wall. Not being able to get into it, he retired to watch those who came out. But the whole day passed away and he saw no one come out.

After sunset he sat down at the entrance of the cavern and kept on watch until midnight; then sleep overcame him.

He was lying with his head on Mimoun's knee, when the latter suddenly awakened him. 'O my master,' said Mimoun, 'I heard some noise in the cavern, and I saw the glimmer of a light.' He rose at once and perceived indeed a light, towards which he went, and which guided him to a recess in the cavern.

He contrived, after much trouble, to reach a kind of crevice, through which the light shone. Looking through it, he saw the princess Zohra, surrounded by about a hundred virgins. They were in a magnificent palace dug out in the heart of the mountain, splendidly furnished and resplendent with gold everywhere. The maidens were eating and drinking and enjoying the pleasures of the table.

Abou el Heïdja said to himself, 'Alas! I have no companion to assist me at this difficult moment.' Under the influence of this reflection he returned to his servant, Mimoun, and said to him, 'Go to my brother before God, Abou el Heïloukh, and tell him to come here to me as quickly as he can.'

When the negro Mimoun came to his master's friend, and told him what had happened, the latter took his sabre, mounted his horse, and taking his favourite negro with him, he made his way, with Mimoun, to the cavern.

Abou el Heïdja bid him welcome, and having informed him of the love he bore to Zohra, told him of his resolution to penetrate forcibly into the palace, and the marvellous scene he had witnessed. Abou el Heïloukh was dumb with surprise.

At nightfall they heard singing, boisterous laughter, and animated talking. Abou el Heïdja said to his friend, 'Go to the end of the subterranean passage and look. You will then make excuse for the love of your brother.' Abou el Heïloukh looked into the interior and was enchanted with the sight of these virgins and their charms. 'O brother,' he asked, 'which among these women is Zohra?'

Abou el Heïdja answered, 'The one with the irreproachable shape, whose smile is irresistible, whose head is encircled by a crown of pearls, and whose garments sparkle with gold. She is seated on a throne incrusted with rare stones and nails of silver, and she is leaning her head upon her hand.'

'I have observed her of all the others,' said Abou el Heïloukh, 'as though she were a blazing torch. But, O my brother, let me draw your attention to a matter which appears not to have struck you. It is very certain that licentiousness reigns in this palace. Observe that these people come here only at night time, and that this is a retired place. There is every reason to believe that it is exclusively consecrated to feasting, drinking, and debauchery. As far as I can see, Zohra solicits the affection of young girls, which is a proof that she can have no inclination for men, nor be responsive to their love.'

'O Abou el Heïloukh,' said Abou el Heïdja, 'I know the value of your judgment. You know that I have never hesitated to follow your advice and counsel!' 'O my brother,' said the son of the Vizir, 'if God had not guided you to this entrance of the palace, you would never have been able to approach Zohra. But from here, please God! we can find our way.'

Next morning, at sunrise, all the four, the two masters and the two servants, entered the cavern and penetrated into the palace, each of them armed with sabre and buckler.

Now they began to explore the palace in every sense. It seemed to them the marvel of marvels. The furniture was magnificent. Everywhere there were beds and couches of all kinds, rich candelabra, splendid lustres, sumptuous carpets, and tables covered with dishes, fruits and beverages.

When they had admired all these treasures, they went on examining the chambers, and in the last found a secret door. They took their position in a cabinet from which one could see without being seen.

So they waited till night came on. At that moment the secret door opened, giving admission to a negress carrying a torch, who set alight all the lustres and candelabra, arranged the beds, set the plates, placed all sorts of meats upon the tables, with cups and bottles, and perfumed the air with the sweetest scents.

Soon afterwards the maidens made their appearance. Their gait denoted at the same time indifference and languor. They seated themselves upon the divans, and the negress offered them meat and drink. They ate, drank, and sang melodiously.

Then the four men, seeing them giddy with wine, came down from their hiding place with their sabres in their hands, brandishing them over the heads of the maidens. They had first taken care to veil their faces with the upper part of their *haïk*.

'Who are these men,' cried Zohra, 'who are invading our dwelling under cover of the night? What do you want?'

'Coition!' they answered.

'With whom?' asked Zohra.

'With you, O apple of my eye!' said Abou el Heïdja.

Zohra: 'Who are you?'

'It is I who met you while out hunting.'

Zohra: 'But what brought you hither?'

'The will of God the Highest!'

At this answer Zohra was silent, and set herself to think of a means by which she could rid herself of these intruders.

Now among the virgins that were present there were several whose vulvas were like iron barred, and whom no one had been able to deflower; there was also present a woman called Mouna who was insatiable as regards coition. Zohra thought to herself, 'It is only by a stratagem I can get rid of these men. By means of these women I will set them tasks which they will be unable to accomplish as conditions for my consent.' Then turning to Abou el Heïdja, she said to him, 'You will not get possession of me unless you fulfil the conditions which I shall impose upon you.' The four cavaliers at once consented to this, and she continued, 'But, if you do not fulfil them, will you pledge your word that you will be my prisoners, and place yourselves entirely at my disposition?' 'We pledge our words!' they answered.

She made them take their oath that they would be faithful to their word, and then, placing her hand in that of Abou el Heïdja, she said to him, 'As regards you, I impose upon you the task of deflowering eighty virgins without ejaculating. Such is my will!'

She let him then enter a chamber where there were several kinds of beds, and sent to him the eighty virgins in succession. Abou el Heïdja deflowered them all, and so ravished in a single night the maidenhood of eighty young girls without ejaculating the smallest drop of sperm. This extraordinary vigour filled Zohra with astonishment, and likewise all those present.

The princess, turning then to the negro Mimoun, said, 'Your task shall be,' pointing to Mouna, 'to do this woman's business without resting for fifty consecutive days; you need not ejaculate unless you like; but if the excess of fatigue forces you to stop, you will not have fulfilled your obligations.' They all cried out at the hardness of such a task; but Mimoun said, 'I accept the condition, and shall come out of it with honour!' The fact was that this negro had an insatiable appetite for the coitus. Zohra told him to go with Mouna to her chamber, impressing upon the latter to let her know if the negro should exhibit the slightest trace of fatigue.

'And you, Abou el Heïloukh, what I require of you is to remain here, in the presence of these women and virgins, for thirty consecutive days, with your member during this period always in erection during day and night.'

Then she said to the fourth. 'You will remain at our disposition for any services which we may have to demand of you.'

However, Zohra, in order to leave no motive for any excuse, had asked them what regimen they wished to follow during their trial. Abou el Heïdja had asked for camel's milk with honey, and chick-peas cooked with meat and onions; and, by means of these aliments he did, by the permission of God, accomplish his remarkable exploit. Abou el Heïloukh demanded onions cooked with meat, and, for drink, the juice pressed out of pounded onions mixed with honey. Mimoun, on his part, asked for yolks of eggs and bread.

However, Abou el Heïdja claimed of Zohra the favour of copulating with her on the strength of the fact that he had fulfilled his engagement. She answered him, 'Oh, impossible! the condition which you have fulfilled is inseparable from those which your companions have to comply with. The agreement must be carried out in its entirety, and you will find me true to my promise. But if one amongst you should fail in his task, you will all be my prisoners by the will of God!'

At first Zohra, feeling convinced that they would soon all be at her mercy, was all amiability and smiles. But when the twentieth day had come she began to show signs of distress; and on the thirtieth she could no longer restrain her tears. For on that day Abou el Heïloukh had finished his task.

From that time the princess, who had now no other hope than in the failure of the negro Mimoun, relied upon his becoming fatigued before he finished his work. She sent every day to Mouna for information, who sent word that the negro's vigor was constantly increasing, and she began to despair. One day she said to the two friends, 'I have made inquiries about the negro, and Mouna has let me know that he was exhausted with fatigue.' At these words Abou el Heïdja cried, 'In the name of God! if he does not carry out his task, aye, and if he does not go beyond it for ten days longer, he shall die the vilest of deaths!'

But his zealous servant never during the period of fifty days took any rest in his work of copulation, and kept going on, besides, for ten days longer, as ordered by his master. Mouna, on her part, had the greatest satisfaction, as this feat had at last appeased her ardour for coition.

Then said Abou el Heïdja to Zohra. 'See, we have fulfilled all the conditions imposed upon us. It is now for you to accord me the favours which was to be the price if we succeeded.' 'It is but too true!' answered the princess, and she gave herself up to him, and he found her excelling the most excellent.

As to the negro, Mimoun, he married Mouna. Abou el Heïloukh chose, amongst all the virgins, the one whom he had found most attractive.

They all remained in the palace, giving themselves up to good cheer and all possible pleasures, until death put an end to their happy existence and dissolved their union. God be merciful to them as well as to all Mussulmans! Amen.

It is to this story that the verses cited previously make allusion. I have given it here, because it testifies to the efficacy of the dishes and remedies, the use of which I have recommended, for giving vigour for coition, and all learned men agree in acknowledging their salutary effects.

> *I certainly did wrong to put this book together;*
> *But you will pardon me, nor let me pray in vain,*
> *O God! award no punishment for this on judgment day!*
> *And thou, oh reader, hear me conjure thee to say: So be it!*

Lightning Source UK Ltd.
Milton Keynes UK
UKHW051627180223
417035UK00044B/226